W9-AEZ-015

DISCARD

Butler Community College
90 South Haverhill Road
El Dorado, Kansas 67042-3280

Butler Community College

3120180845

IT HAPPENED TO ME

Series Editor: Arlene Hirschfelder

Books in the It Happened to Me series are designed for inquisitive teens digging for answers about certain illnesses, social issues, or lifestyle interests. Whether you are deep into your teen years or just entering them, these books are gold mines of up-to-date information, riveting teen views, and great visuals to help you figure out stuff. Besides special boxes highlighting singular facts, each book is enhanced with the latest reading lists, websites, and an index. Perfect for browsing, there are loads of expert information by acclaimed writers to help parents, guardians, and librarians understand teen illness, tough situations, and lifestyle choices.

1. *Epilepsy: The Ultimate Teen Guide*, by Kathlyn Gay and Sean McGarrahan, 2002.
2. *Stress Relief: The Ultimate Teen Guide*, by Mark Powell, 2002.
3. *Learning Disabilities: The Ultimate Teen Guide*, by Penny Hutchins Paquette and Cheryl Gerson Tuttle, 2003.
4. *Making Sexual Decisions: The Ultimate Teen Guide*, by L. Kris Gowen, 2003.
5. *Asthma: The Ultimate Teen Guide*, by Penny Hutchins Paquette, 2003.
6. *Cultural Diversity—Conflicts and Challenges: The Ultimate Teen Guide*, by Kathlyn Gay, 2003.
7. *Diabetes: The Ultimate Teen Guide*, by Katherine J. Moran, 2004.
8. *When Will I Stop Hurting? Teens, Loss, and Grief: The Ultimate Teen Guide to Dealing with Grief*, by Ed Myers, 2004.
9. *Volunteering: The Ultimate Teen Guide*, by Kathlyn Gay, 2004.
10. *Organ Transplants—A Survival Guide for the Entire Family: The Ultimate Teen Guide*, by Tina P. Schwartz, 2005.
11. *Medications: The Ultimate Teen Guide*, by Cheryl Gerson Tuttle, 2005.
12. *Image and Identity—Becoming the Person You Are: The Ultimate Teen Guide*, by L. Kris Gowen and Molly C. McKenna, 2005.
13. *Apprenticeship: The Ultimate Teen Guide*, by Penny Hutchins Paquette, 2005.
14. *Cystic Fibrosis: The Ultimate Teen Guide*, by Melanie Ann Apel, 2006.
15. *Religion and Spirituality in America: The Ultimate Teen Guide*, by Kathlyn Gay, 2006.

DEALING
WITH DEATH

THE ULTIMATE TEEN GUIDE

KATHLYN GAY

IT HAPPENED TO ME, NO. 55

ROWMAN & LITTLEFIELD
Lanham • Boulder • New York • London

Published by Rowman & Littlefield
A wholly owned subsidiary of The Rowman & Littlefield Publishing Group, Inc.
4501 Forbes Boulevard, Suite 200, Lanham, Maryland 20706
www.rowman.com

Unit A, Whitacre Mews, 26-34 Stannary Street, London SE11 4AB

Copyright © 2017 by Rowman & Littlefield

All rights reserved. No part of this book may be reproduced in any form or by any electronic
or mechanical means, including information storage and retrieval systems, without written
permission from the publisher, except by a reviewer who may quote passages in a review.

British Library Cataloguing in Publication Information Available

Library of Congress Cataloging-in-Publication Data

Names: Gay, Kathlyn, author.
Title: Dealing with death : the ultimate teen guide / Kathlyn Gay.
Description: Lanham, Maryland : Rowman & Littlefield, [2017] | Series: It happened to me ;
    No. 55 | Includes bibliographical references and index.
Identifiers: LCCN 2017017503 (print) | LCCN 2017038494 (ebook) | ISBN 9781538102756
    (electronic) | ISBN 9781538102749 (hardback : alk. paper)
Subjects: LCSH: Death. | Loss (Psychology) | Teenagers and death.
Classification: LCC HQ1073 (ebook) | LCC HQ1073 .G39 2017 (print) | DDC 306.9—dc23
LC record available at https://lccn.loc.gov/2017017503

∞™ The paper used in this publication meets the minimum requirements of American
National Standard for Information Sciences—Permanence of Paper for Printed Library
Materials, ANSI/NISO Z39.48-1992.

Printed in the United States of America

To my children and grand children
with the hope that all will have
healthy and meaningful lives

Contents

Acknowledgments

While death is often stressful to write and talk about, many people have shared in print, online, and in person their thoughts, sorrows, and insights about death in their lives. I appreciate all the comments, especially the words of terminally ill or injured young people—they have helped shape this book. And thank you to all the readers who have been willing to explore the reality of death and how many of us face and grieve the loss of family, friends, and beloved companion animals.

DEATH IN YOUR LIFE

"When reality hits me that I will die one day I get stricken with this feeling of doom and really intense depression. I'll start imagining certain scenarios and how awful it would be if I died this way or that way. I don't know why I do it and it happens quite often."—Jocelyn, TeenHelp.org[1]

Death. The very word can invoke mental pictures of skull and crossbones, human skeletons, the Grim Reaper, cadavers, or other spooky images. Some people are frightened just reading about death. Or the subject may seem creepy or morbid or downright depressing.

It's common for people to have anxieties about the death of those they love or their own death. One young adult noted in an online post, "I get anxiety thinking about it. Does anyone else have this fear? That you are just afraid to die? I hate thinking about it but sometimes i [*sic*] can't help myself and i get really worked up over it."[2]

On the same website a young man named Jake wrote,

I'm not going to lie, I'm absolutely terrified of dying. I try not to think about it too much though because if I let myself think about it in too much depth then I end up getting really upset over it. I hate the thought that when you die that's it, there is nothing and you'll never come back. However, I think you just have to try and not think about it too much because life is too short to worry about something that is going to happen to everybody at one point or another. You just have to try and live life to the full and enjoy every single day.[3]

The authors of *The Art of Dying: Honoring and Celebrating Life's Passages* underscore these posts. "In this society, the ultimate fear is the fear of death," they wrote. "This fear can infiltrate your entire being, trample your spirit, rob you of your joy and passion. Fear of death is especially painful because we do not

A skull and crossbones is one of the common images that come to mind when people think or talk about death. © iStock.com/vladru

acknowledge it. Death is so taboo, so mysterious, so outside our day-to-day lives, that we act as if it isn't part of our life cycle."[4]

Thanatophobia

It's a tongue-twisting word that means fear of death—a persistent and sometimes unreasonable fear. "This fear may itself be related to other fears, including those based on religious beliefs and fear of the unknown," wrote Lisa Fritscher in a blog post about thanatophobia on the website VeryWell.com. "Some fear the act of dying, while others fret about what may occur beyond the moment of death." Fritscher pointed out that thanatophobia "is a relatively complicated phobia. . . . Many, if not most, people are afraid of dying. However, if the fear is so prevalent as to affect your daily life, then you might have a full-blown phobia."[5]

Most people do not suffer from a death phobia, but the subject is not an easy conversational topic for teens and young adults, or older adults for that matter. It is not unusual for teenagers to try to overcome "feelings of vulnerability and powerlessness by engag[ing] in risk-taking behavior to enjoy the thrilling relief of survival," wrote Robert Kastenbaum for DeathReference.com. Or teens "dive into horror movies and other expressions of bizarre and violent death; indulge in computerized games whose object is to destroy targeted beings; and/or try to impersonate" death as goths. In other words, "It is safer to act as though one were already nearly dead and therefore harmless. Death need not bother with a creature that seems to have so little life."[6]

Denial of Death

Death has always been a touchy subject, whether due to fear, superstition, or discomfort at the prospect of mortality. It's often a taboo subject in families, schools, and communities, and most Americans seldom express their attitudes and feelings about death—a kind of rejection or denial that life eventually ends.

Denial of death is a term first coined by the founder of psychoanalysis, Sigmund Freud, in a 1915 essay on people's attitudes toward death. Freud wrote his essay six months after the start of World War I. He claimed that people could no longer deny death because they were faced with thousands being killed each day. Since Freud's time, hundreds of millions have died in wars and other catastrophes, yet there has not been a change in the way individuals view death.

During the American Civil War, photographs of the dead showed soldiers stacked liked cords of wood. But in much later times, war news shown on television frequently seemed to be more like a video game or movie—not quite real and devoid of actual death.

Critics of a sanitized war contend that the blood, gore, and horror need to be shown in order to bring home the point that war is hell and people die. In fact, that is what happened during the Vietnam War, when "images of thousands of dead U.S. soldiers helped to turn the tide of public opinion against the Vietnam War," according to DemocracyNow.com. However, during the war in Iraq in 2003, Western news coverage seldom included photographs of corpses of soldiers or citizens, and by 2005, photojournalists were "banned from military funerals at Arlington National Cemetery." And the *Los Angeles Times* documented that photos of American casualties were rarely published "in six

Death Superstitions

Nearly every culture holds superstitious beliefs, among them omens about impending death and superstitions about funerals, burials, and graves. Numerous superstitions focus on the deceased. For example, one common superstition worldwide requires that doors and windows be left open to allow the deceased's spirit to escape. A dead person should be carried out of a house feet first so that the deceased's spirit will not look back and signal others to go to their deaths as well. Eyes of the deceased must be closed, or they will look for the next person to die. Another says that flowers growing on a grave indicate the deceased led a good life, while weeds covering a grave indicate the deceased was evil.

A common superstition around the world is that a wild bird flying into a home or pecking on a window signifies that someone in a family will soon die. In many cultures, the hoot of an owl or bark of a dog at midnight is supposed to portend death. A sharp knife, such as a kitchen knife, should never be given as a gift, the superstitious say, because the recipient of such a gift will have her or his life cut short. A mirror falling off the wall and breaking is a sign that there will soon be a death in the household. In addition, when someone dies, the clock in the home should be stopped, but no one explains why.

According to other superstitions, death may also occur soon in a family if someone puts his or her shoes on the bed, takes a photograph of a deceased family member, wears something new to a funeral, holds a funeral on a Friday or on a rainy day, or if a stopped clock suddenly begins working. Dropping an umbrella on the floor foretells a murder in the house.

There are several versions of a superstition that tell what a person is supposed to do when a hearse goes by or when one passes a cemetery. Superstitious people hold their breath and close their eyes to keep death away or to prevent spirits from entering their bodies.

major newspapers during a six month period. Readers of the *Atlanta Journal-Constitution*, *Los Angeles Times*, *New York Times*, *St. Louis Post–Dispatch* and *Washington Post* never saw a single picture of a dead serviceman or servicewoman in their morning papers."[7]

Because of war, death has become part of the life experience in some parts of the world. In war-torn countries children grow up exposed to death; they also face starvation, poor health conditions, and short life spans. In some areas of urban America, death may be seen as "the way life is" because killings are common occurrences or poverty thwarts efforts to maintain good health and a long life.

Impoverished people (many of them children and adolescents) face early death for many reasons. They are often unable to afford medical care, nutritious food, safe housing, and education to obtain a higher standard of living. Obesity and diabetes are major killers of poor people, although the middle class and affluent are also affected with these health problems.

However, a majority of young people (primarily white Anglo Americans) are sheltered from death when their families are healthy. Funerals of young family members are rare, and seldom is death a topic of discussion. "America is a youth culture that emphasizes beauty, virility, ambition and athletic prowess," wrote author Elliot Essman, on LifeintheUSA.com. Essman added, "Within this culture, aging, decline, and death are things that happen to other people, preferably in other countries, but not to us, the type of thing we see on television but rarely stare in the face. We keep death at a distance. Death is for the very old who have used up their allotment of life. . . . Only when death hits the young do we have a truly tragic understanding of the event."[8]

Euphemisms for Death

To say simply that someone has died seems harsh or awkward in many circumstances. Thus, people have invented numerous words or phrases that mean the same thing. In other words they use euphemisms, or indirect expressions that replace words and phrases considered harsh or taboo. The deceased, for example, are called the departed and are laid to rest rather than buried. People near death—about to die—are referred to as terminally ill. Those who euthanize their pets by injection are likely to say they had them put to sleep.

When people speak of a death, they may use a more neutral expression implying mere transition, as in saying the person passed away, passed on, crossed over, expired, or went to the big mansion in the sky. Or they say a person bit the dust, cashed in his chips, gave up the ghost, departed this life, or kicked the bucket. The latter may refer to an old English practice of hanging a slaughtered animal

Death in Literature and Art

In spite of the fact that the reality of death is often denied, high school and college students may be exposed to many representations of death—some of them brutal—in literature and art. Death, particularly murder, is at the core of the literary form known as the tragedy. Murders motivated by fate, stupidity, or revenge fill the first tragedies of ancient Greek dramas.

In later times, authors known for their preoccupation with death include Americans Edgar Allan Poe (1809–1849) and Ambrose Bierce (1842–1914). Poe, in his "The Philosophy of Composition" (1846), declares the most universally appreciable subject of beauty to be "the death of a beautiful woman," a theory that no doubt reflected the long illness and death of his own wife, Virginia, and that Poe put into practice in numerous works, such as "The Raven," "The Fall of the House of Usher," and "Ligeia." Bierce, meanwhile, was concerned in his short stories with deriving horror from the physical presence of a corpse itself in a room, his characters often being driven mad due to the mere proximity of a dead body, a theme that perhaps derives from Bierce's own Civil War battlefield experiences.

Since the twentieth century, the Gothic genre has been represented in mystery and horror novels. The horror novel is concerned mainly with the immortal, spiritual facet of death (ghosts and the afterlife), while the mystery novel is mainly a "who done it"—dealing with murder, the condition of the corpse, and finding the killer.

Samuel Beckett, who won the 1969 Nobel Prize in literature, saw life as futile, a matter of waiting to die. In his well-known play *Waiting for Godot*, Beckett poses the unanswerable question: what is the purpose of life? His play maintains that life is meaningless and depends on chance, but humans try to find direction by inventing illusions or patterns in order to survive.

The representation of death in the visual arts has a long history. Images of battle and suffering fill numerous paintings by well-known artists. The famous Spanish-born artist Pablo Picasso (1881–1973), for example, created a masterpiece about war, a huge mural called *Guernica*. It was inspired by the German bombing of the peaceful Basque village of Guernica in northern Spain during the Spanish Civil War. Nazi Germany and fascist Italy supported the Nationalists, or rebels, during the war. Guernica held out against the Nationalists, so at the request of Spanish Nationalist commander General Emilio Mola, Nazi Germany, led by Hitler, bombed the peaceful village over a two-hour period, killing more than 1,600 people and injuring hundreds of others.

A tapestry depicting a reproduction of *Guernica* hangs in the United Nations (UN) Building in New York City. But in 2003, when U.S. secretary of state Colin Powell went to the UN to make his case for war with Iraq, UN officials placed a blue cover over the tapestry, claiming the scene of war's horror sent a mixed message.

from a beam or yoke that was called a bucket. The dead animal, usually a pig, had spasms after it died and kicked against the bucket—hence the saying.

Euphemisms for death may be religious in nature; for example, he met St. Peter, she went to her heavenly reward, they met their Maker, he knocked at the pearly gates, or they crossed the River Jordan.

There is also a whole category of euphemisms for killing people. For example, someone who died of electrocution was fried or became toast. Among criminals who commit murder, the terms used include iced, whacked, or terminated. The phrase *sleeps with the fishes* denotes a murdered person whose corpse was disposed of in a body of water.

Bought the farm is a euphemism from World War I soldiers, who, at a time when the population of the United States was mostly rural, all dreamed of returning safely home to their own farmland. Thus, when a comrade died, his friends would say he had at last bought the farm.

In the modern U.S. military, civilians who are killed in combat are referred to as collateral damage. Bodies of military personnel who die in battle are sent home in human remains pouches, a euphemism that gained general usage in 1991.

Even though most people do not like to talk about death in a realistic fashion, it is a topic covered profusely in modern media, whether in movies and television or obituaries and news stories about real people who have died. The preponderance of death in the media has some sociologists suggesting that Americans, whether young or old, have become blasé about death and dying. In other words, death has become so common that some people are indifferent and view death as simply part of life.

Yet it is important to face the reality of death, primarily because it is inevitable—it will happen to all of us. Talking or reading about death can be helpful when individuals have to deal with their own imminent death or the death of loved ones. Today in the United States, numerous professionals—counselors, psychologists, health-care personnel, hospice workers, religious leaders—are engaged in efforts to help individuals with death and dying. As Essman put it, "Pushing death aside may have its benefits for the young, but it short-circuits the natural human need to come to terms with the effect death has on us, whether our own deaths or the deaths of those we love."[9]

Facing Death in the Past

In early America, people were more *personally* associated with death than they are today. Most people lived on farms and were connected in some way with the natural cycles of plant life and the birth, growth, and death of animals. Death was also an ever-present factor in many families, because diseases such as tuberculosis, diphtheria, cholera, and yellow fever killed people of all ages. Women frequently died in childbirth, and the death of newborns was common.

Americans also faced death because of numerous wars throughout the nation's history. In the American Revolution (1775–1783) there were 4,435 battle deaths. In the War of 1812 (1812–1815) and the Mexican War (1846–1848), nearly 4,000 soldiers died. The (American) Indian wars (1817–1898) resulted in 1,000 battle deaths, according to the U.S. Department of Veterans Affairs.[10]

More soldiers—Union and Confederate—died in the Civil War (1861–1865) than in all the previous armed conflicts combined. "Approximately 620,000 soldiers died from combat, accident, starvation, and disease during the Civil War. A recent study puts the number of dead as high as 850,000," according to the Civil War Trust.[11]

Whatever the risks to life, Americans in the 1800s and early 1900s lived an average of forty to forty-seven years. In spite of wars, most people died at home. The deceased were often laid out in the family living room where relatives and friends gathered to share their grief. Death, in short, was a common occurrence in everyday life. People may have feared dying but knew they had to persevere regardless.

Currently, at least 80 percent of Americans would prefer that their last days be spent at home, but most terminally ill patients die in hospitals or other health-care institutions. Increasingly people are expressing concern about where they will die. When a dying person is cared for at home, he or she will probably experience more peace, but family members may be overwhelmed. Home care for a terminally ill family member becomes a long vigil for the caregivers. Some

A young widow of the 1800s is depicted at a grave site, mourning her husband's death. © iStock.com/Studio-Annika

Death Cafes

A Death Cafe is an event, an occasion in which people get together over tea and cake (or other food) to discuss the reality of death. Groups do not focus on grief or bereavement counseling. Rather their "objective is to increase awareness of death with a view to helping people make the most of their (finite) lives," according to DeathCafe.com. The purpose is to weave the taboo topic into everyday conversations.[a]

The first discussion group was organized in September 2011 by Jon Underwood of London and held in the basement of his home. "When people sit down to talk about death, the pretense kind of falls away, and people talk very openly and authentically," Underwood says. "And they say things in front of strangers which are really profound and beautiful. And for English people to do that, with our traditional stiff upper lip, is very rare."[b]

Since 2011, Underwood's idea has spread worldwide. By January 2017, there had been 3,983 Death Cafes in forty-two countries, from Argentina to Zimbabwe. A number of events were held in such diverse U.S. places as San Rafael, California; White River Junction, Vermont; the Denver area, Colorado; southern Maryland; East Windsor, New Jersey; Bellingham, Washington; Santa Barbara, California; Corvallis, Oregon; Apache Junction, Arizona; and many other communities.

"When we acknowledge that we're going to die, it falls back on ourselves to ask the question, 'in this limited time that I've got, what's important for me to do?'" Underwood explained in a 2013 interview with NPR.[c]

families may seek advice on how to take on caregiver responsibilities. They may find helpful information in books or on the Internet or from professionals who provide hospice care at home. Hospice care is a topic discussed later in this book.

Attitudes about Death

As noted, the common American attitude toward death includes fear, denial, and avoidance. However, those outlooks vary with individuals and have been changing somewhat with death and dying education that began around the 1960s and 1970s with such leaders as Dr. Jeanne Quint Benoliel (1919–2012), who is known for her research on how one learns to live with chronic and/or terminal illness; Dame Cicely Saunders (1918–2005), a British woman who founded the first modern hospice; and Elisabeth Kübler-Ross (1926–2004), who taught a seminar on death and dying in a Chicago hospital, helping to overcome a "conspiracy of silence" regarding the terminally ill. Her ground-breaking book *On Death and Dying* (1969) describes how patients deal with death and has been read and studied ever since by countless health-care providers as well as people in other walks of life.

Traditionally, physicians and other health-care professionals have avoided discussions of end-of-life issues with terminally ill patients and their families, because they frequently consider death a medical failure. But over the past few decades some medical schools and other institutions have offered classes in death education. In addition some universities are implementing courses that educate resident doctors on, for example, how to communicate with parents whose children are terminally ill, how to explain to patients that they are nearing death, and how to talk to patients about advance directives and other end-of-life concerns. Death and dying education courses may also include a study of contemporary attitudes regarding death and dying; the physiological, sociological, and psychological effects of dying; bereavement, grief, and mourning; medical ethics; and violent deaths.

Over the years, published and electronic materials have theorized that individuals can prepare for their own or someone else's death by changing their attitudes about death, dying, and bereavement, which, the experts contend, are learned through a culture. Thus a death-denying attitude may be unlearned, and death can be accepted as a reality of life. Some of the steps toward that end include developing a positive attitude about self while living; looking honestly at the fears one has about death; talking about death; and making specific practical arrangements for the end of life, such as advance directives and funeral and burial options. "Advance directives aren't just for older adults," the Mayo Clinic points out. "Unexpected end-of-life situations can happen at any age, so it's important for all adults to prepare these documents."[12] That advice applies to teenagers as well.

Courses on death and bereavement are currently being offered at undergraduate schools and universities. Authors of a popular textbook used in college courses on death and bereavement write,

> Studying death, dying, and bereavement quickly discloses that we are in fact finite, limited beings. This realization clearly impacts on how we live our lives, for we learn that although there are many things in life that we can control, there are many others that we cannot. Death-related education

reveals some specific things we can *control*, even as it shows many of the *limitations* that make our control less than complete . . . in the end it is always an individual person who must deal with these particularized experiences: no one else can die our death or experience our grief. [13]

The authors also emphasize that "life can be good even though it is transient" and that learning about death provides opportunities to seek inspiration and to "maximize our lives." [14]

Death education (or death ed) is a particular passion for Dr. Jessica Nutic Jitter, a critical care specialist in Oakland, California. She cares for patients in Highland Hospital's intensive care unit (ICU) where many terminal patients are kept alive with medical machinery. Dr. Jitter believes teenagers especially need knowledge about death. She explained, "Every year in my I.C.U. I see dozens of young people at the bedsides of dying relatives. If we started to teach death ed in high school, a student visiting a dying grandparent might draw from the curriculum to ask a question that could shift the entire conversation. She might ask about a palliative care consultation, for example, or share important information about the patient's preferences that she elicited during her course. High school, when students are getting their drivers' licenses and considering organ donation, is the perfect time for this. Where else do we have the attention of our entire society?" [15]

Dr. Jitter argues that death education should be taught in all high schools. In an article for the *New York Times*, she noted that she and a colleague Dawn Gross taught their first death ed class in February 2017. "We described the realities of life in the I.C.U. without mincing words—the effects of a life prolonged on machines, the arm restraints, the isolation. Everyone was with us, a little tentative, but rapt." She concluded, "No one had fainted. No one had run out of the class screaming. . . . It is my hope that this is only the first step toward generating wide public literacy about this phase of life, which will eventually affect us all. The sooner we start talking about it, the better." [16]

WHEN SOMEONE CLOSE DIES

....

"When my friend died, the rest of the world kept going and no one knew
what I was going through."—a teenager on the Grief Healing *blog*[1]

D eath cannot be ignored when it strikes close to home. Whether by accident, violence, or disease, the death of family members or friends can be heartbreaking for the living. If you have experienced the death of a friend, family member, or classmate, you may feel not only grief but also helplessness, as if you cannot cope with death. It is common for young people to grieve deeply but try to hide their feelings and look for diversions. It's not unusual to appear nonchalant while churning inside. Sometimes people react with anger and begin acting recklessly, using drugs, or acting out in some other way. Some people question their faith, or they may withdraw from social activities. Others try to ease the pain by posting on various social media.

On the *Grief Healing* blog, a teenager lamented: "No one could understand the pain I was feeling. I wanted the world to stop and I wanted to just scream out, 'Doesn't anyone realize that I am hurt?' I kept looking at people and thinking, 'You don't have a care, and look at me, one of my friends just died.'"[2]

After his friend committed suicide, teenager Zach described his reaction on a teen suicide prevention website: "When I got to school and heard the news, I thought they were kidding. It was too bizarre to believe. When I realized they couldn't be so sick to make up a joke that Mike was gone, I believed it—sorta. But I got to tell you, even though I saw his body at the funeral and all, sometimes it still seems not real to me."[3]

A Blog about Grief and Healing

Grief counselor and nurse Marty Tousley produces a blog that can be found at GriefHealingBlog.com. She was a bereavement counselor at Hospice of the Valley in Phoenix, Arizona, for seventeen years and for ten of those years was moderator for its innovative online grief healing discussion groups. In 2013, she took ownership of the online site and invited grieving people of all ages to write to her, whether mourning a deceased loved one or companion animal. One example is an anonymous girl who describes the grief she experienced when a friend drowned:

> It has been 1 year and 2 months and I am still grieving like crazy, people say it gets easier but it hasn't. I miss her like crazy. To me, it feels as if it were yesterday that I was looking at her smiling face. . . . Even when I see certain things or her name I sometimes break out crying. I can't seem to move on and recently I got into an argument with someone who told me that I have no clue about death and that I should get over it.[a]

On the same blog, a teenager had this to say about her father's death:

> I feel really sad sometimes, because I miss my dad. I was very close to him, and we were very alike in the way we were both mechanical. He was a professor of engineering and he wrote many articles and textbooks. I am very proud of him. I boast about him a lot. . . . It's just gone past 6 months since he died, and I'm beginning to feel very sad a lot of the time.[b]

Many more readers write to Tousley about their grief, and she responds with counseling and condolences. The blog also lists websites that provide advice and help for teens who are grieving.

If one of your friends died, you would probably feel devastated. © iStock.com/StphaneLemire

Deaths from Accidents and Gun Violence

Unfortunately news stories about teen deaths are probably familiar to you. Vehicle crashes have long been the leading cause of teen deaths. In 2014, the Centers for Disease Control and Prevention (CDC) reported that "2,270 teens in the United States ages 16–19 were killed and 221,313 were treated in emergency departments for injuries suffered in motor vehicle crashes. That means that six teens ages 16–19 died every day from motor vehicle injuries."[4]

Teens in vehicle crashes often are distracted by the use of their cell phones or by drinking or eating while driving. Speeding or other risky driving is another cause of deadly teen accidents. And alcohol and substance abuse also are to blame for teen vehicle deaths.

In June 2016, two Texas teenagers were killed in a car accident caused by a twenty-three-year-old drunk driver. One of the teens killed was Bailee Russell, who had just attended her high school graduation; the other was Haley Johnson, a student at Stephen F. Austin State University. "It was devastating," Bailee's friend said after learning of the tragedy. "It was hard to believe. It's still hard to believe. It doesn't feel real."[5]

Another top teen killer is gun violence. "Homicide is the leading cause of death for non-Hispanic black male teenagers," according to the CDC.[6] During just one week in early November 2016, seven teenagers were shot and killed in cities across the United States. During that same period, many others were injured due to gun violence. "Every day, 48 children and teens are shot in murders, assaults, suicides and suicide attempts, unintentional shootings, and police intervention." On an annual basis that number totals 17,383 children and teens killed or wounded because of gun violence, according to the Brady Campaign to Prevent Gun Violence.[7]

Cancer Deaths

Cancer is also one of the leading causes of teen death. Zach Sobiech of Stillwater, Montana, was one teenager who died of the disease. When he was fourteen, he was diagnosed with osteosarcoma, a bone cancer, and was told that he probably had less than a year to live. As a way to say goodbye, Zach, a guitarist, wrote and performed songs. He wrote about facing death in his song "Clouds." At first he shared it only with family and friends, and later released it on YouTube in 2012. Millions viewed the performance and sang the lyrics that tell about falling into "a dark hole" and flying up into the clouds where there is a better view. You can read the lyrics on the Internet and hear the song on YouTube.[8]

Zach celebrated his eighteenth birthday on May 3, 2016, and died seventeen days later. Since Zach's death, celebrities have honored him by lip-synching or

Using a cell phone while driving is the cause of many vehicle accidents. © iStock.com/encrier

playing his song. During the Christmas holidays, thousands of people have gathered at the Mall of America near Minneapolis and St. Paul, Minnesota, to sing "Clouds" and raise awareness for the Children's Cancer Research Fund that provides 100 percent of its donations to osteosarcoma research.

Canadian Laura Hiller of Ontario was another teen diagnosed with cancer—acute myeloid leukemia, which spreads quickly. She was only thirteen years old at the time and struggled with the disease for years. In mid-2015, she learned she had a donor for a bone marrow transplant. But there were many people ahead of her waiting for transplants and no hospital beds were available. She died in January 2016 before she could have life-saving surgery. She was eighteen years old.

Laura's friends and family reacted to her untimely death in a dramatic way. Classmates signed her casket just as they would have done in her high school yearbook. With colored markers some signers inked in musical notes, representing Laura's love of musical dramas. One message said, "Life Is a Song . . . Sing 'til your heart's content." Photos published in the *Daily Mail* show Laura's casket covered almost completely with blue, red, and green messages.[9]

Death from Eating Disorders

Many teen deaths occur because of psychological problems, such as eating disorders. If you know a friend or family member who has an eating disorder such as anorexia or bulimia, you may be aware that she or he is risking health problems and perhaps even death. Although not a leading cause of death for young people in the United States, eating disorders affect both males and females who are dissatisfied with their body size and shape.

Girls and young women are more likely to have eating disorders that lead to death. "For females between fifteen to twenty-four years old who suffer from anorexia nervosa, the mortality rate associated with the illness is twelve times higher than the death rate of all other causes of death," according to the National Eating Disorders Association (NEDA). Psychiatric eating disorders like anorexia or bulimia may "occur with one or more other psychiatric disorders" such as alcohol or substance abuse or depression, "which can complicate treatment and make recovery more difficult," NEDA reported.[10]

People who suffer from anorexia refuse to eat, and when they do eat, they consume little and sometimes vomit or use laxatives to purge themselves. Bulimics often are binge eaters, gorging on meals, but they vomit their food in order to lose weight. People with either disorder do not get sufficient nutrients and lack the electrolytes essential for many body functions, especially the heart.

One example is a teenager from Longview, Texas, who died in 2015 due to her eating disorder. Lacey Smarr was a high school freshman and had been a member of her eighth-grade volleyball team. When her friends teased her about her physical appearance in her volleyball uniform, saying her "butt looked fat," Lacey took the teasing seriously. She thought she was getting fat. She began eating healthy foods and running daily with her stepfather, James Miller. She was "losing weight but still eating," Miller told a reporter. They stopped working out but "it got worse," he said. [11]

Off the Bookshelf

The book *34 Pieces of You* by Carmen Rodrigues is a somber, tragic, and somewhat raw story about drug use and abuse that leads to suicide attempts and finally death from a drug overdose. It also deals with cutting, bullying, and homosexuality, as well as unsuspecting or somewhat indifferent parents.

The novel begins with a chilling discovery of two teens in the hospital—Ellie and Sarah, who have overdosed on pills and alcohol. Ellie is dead but Sarah survives. Narrators in the novel are Ellie's brother Jake, Ellie's friend Sarah, and Sarah's younger sister Jessie. Although Ellie is no longer alive, her story is revealed as the three narrators recall various times before and after Ellie's death, slowly revealing hints about her life. Ellie has written down secrets of her life on pieces of paper hidden in a shoebox stuffed under her bed.

In the story Ellie is a complex character, sometimes caustic and mean, other times caring and fun loving. After Ellie dies, Jake, Sarah, and Jessie try to understand and deal with guilt and grief. Jake regrets ignoring his sister's calls for help. Sarah is haunted with guilt for not stopping the drug abuse and for surviving death, a guilt that sends her into a clinical depression. Sarah's younger sister Jessie has had a sexual relationship with Ellie but cannot tell anyone about it and has no one to help her grieve. The novel, which pulls the reader along with hints about Ellie's disturbing life, finally alludes to what has happened yet does not actually explain with details. Yet it is clear that Sarah, Jake, and Jessie must deal with Ellie's death. How they do that is what this book is about. It is also about the need to pay attention if friends show signs of abuse and/or depression that could lead to death.

Unbeknownst to her parents, Lacey was eating and then going to the bathroom to throw up her food. One day she fainted and hit her head. Her parents took her to a doctor, who found no evidence of an eating disorder. But she dropped from 126 pounds in eighth grade to 88 pounds when she entered Longview Global High School as a freshman.

On February 2, 2015, Lacey left school, complaining that she did not feel well. At home, her stepfather found her unconscious. Miller tried to revive her, but Lacey had suffered a heart attack due to her eating disorder. Her body lacked the nutrients needed for her survival.

Candy Miller, Lacey's mother, obviously was devastated. She blamed herself for not recognizing Lacey's problem and assured her daughter's friends that their teasing was not responsible. Lacey had been able to hide her disorder from everyone. In March 2015, Candy Miller announced that she was starting the Lacey Foundation to raise awareness of eating disorders. She explained to a reporter, "I feel like if we can save just one family from the grief we're going through and the pain, then my daughter didn't die in vain."[12]

Today, there is life-saving help for the many who suffer from anorexia in the United States and other industrialized nations. Books and Internet sites address the issue, and aid is provided by organizations such as Alliance for Eating Disorders, Binge Eating Disorder Association, Eating Disorder Foundation, National Association of Anorexia Nervosa and Associated Disorders, and NEDA.

Elisabeth Kübler-Ross and Five Stages of Grief

As many people have noted, dealing with grief following the death of someone close is difficult to say the least. Many people over decades have turned for advice to Dr. Elisabeth Kübler-Ross, whose books are well known for defining the five stages of grief: denial and isolation, anger, bargaining, depression, and acceptance. She defined these stages after conducting a series of interviews with patients who had been diagnosed with illnesses that were often terminal. These interviews first included a small group of young people, and then a larger group of students listening behind a one-way mirror. Her findings are detailed in the book *On Death and Dying*, first published in 1969 and republished in numerous editions since.

Although originally the five stages were related specifically to people coming to terms with their own potentially fatal illnesses, over the decades psychologists have recognized the stages are similar in any strong experience of loss, such as divorce. (Some people who have divorced insist that it is like experiencing a death.)

Kübler-Ross argued that a person who was dying, given sufficient time, would experience each of the stages in order—beginning with denial and ending with acceptance. However, despite the linear progression of the stages, they are not mutually exclusive and patients do move back and forth between the stages.

The first stage, denial, is marked by a refusal to admit to the severity of the illness. Interestingly, denial is not related to whether patients are told directly or whether they have deduced the severity of their illness. Kübler-Ross insisted that people should not be told of their diagnosis in such a way as to leave no hope, since no one can really claim to know the outcome or how long a terminal person may linger. In her view it is best to be direct about the diagnosis, but to keep the door open for the possible effectiveness of treatment routes or the discovery of new cures. In this way, the doctor respects the patient's right to come to terms with the diagnosis in time.

Once patients have moved past "Not me," they ask angrily, "Why me?" This anger is frequently directed at anyone and everyone—family, caregivers, God (if they believe in God), a healthy person who can do something the patient cannot, or even an older unhealthy person who is perceived to be more deserving of dying. This stage can be particularly difficult for the people who are close to the patient. If they can stop themselves from taking the anger personally, it may be easier for the patient to become more rational. When people withdraw from patients because they are angry, this only makes the sick ones feel more insignificant and lonely.

In her book, Kübler-Ross suggested part of the reason for patients' anger may be a loss of control over their bodies, their activities, their very lives. She advocates that caregivers and families be sensitive to offering choices so patients can at least control small things like when their bedding is changed or when visitors come to see them.

After anger, patients move to the third stage: bargaining. This is where they make promises to be good in some way to earn more time or be able to accomplish something they desire. Kübler-Ross noted that some patients may promise to devote their lives to God or to serve the church if they are allowed to live. In effect, bargaining is an effort to postpone the outcome.

Psychologically, because guilt may be associated with bargaining, Kübler-Ross advocated a multidisciplinary approach to treating patients facing death. When patients discover bargaining does not work, they become depressed, which is the fourth stage. Depression may arise because of all the losses patients are enduring—decreased physical activity, financial constraints of expensive treatments, and knowing that they will not be alive to help raise children. Or terminally ill patients may experience depression as they prepare for actually leaving the world.

Reaching the final stage, acceptance, is not the same as being happy about one's death. Instead, there is an absence of emotional pain, as well as other feelings. Patients tend to detach themselves from those closest to them, as if in preparation to leave this world. Kübler-Ross notes that this is often when the family is most in need of support and understanding. The patient may become less interested in the outside world, in talking, and in having visitors. Communication may shift to more nonverbal expressions like holding hands quietly.

To the patient, finally, death is viewed as a relief, which sometimes can be hard for the family to understand. Sometimes the family's need to hang on to a dying patient makes it difficult for them to hear what the person's needs are. Patients may ask their family to let them go. In these last hours of life, patients may reach a "silence that goes beyond words" and achieve a peaceful death.[13]

After defining the five stages of grief, Kübler-Ross went on to write other books on related topics: *Live until We Say Goodbye* (1978), *Living with Death and Dying* (1981), and *On Children and Death: How Children and Their Parents Can and Do Cope with Death* (1997). The latter book describes her work with dying children and provides help and comforting advice for parents and siblings of terminally ill young people in their family. Her final book *On Grief and Grieving: Finding the Meaning of Grief through the Five Stages of Loss* was written with David Kessler in 2004 and published in 2005 after Kübler-Ross's death.

The Risk and Reality of Death in Military Families

In 2011 "more than 1.2 million dependent children lived in active-duty [military] families, and 409,801 spouses and 743,736 dependent children lived in Guard and Reserve families," reported Molly Clever and David R. Segal in a 2013 issue of *The Future of Children*, a journal published by Princeton University and the Brookings Institution. According to the authors, since 1973 when the military became an all-volunteer service, leaders have understood that "whether service members decide to reenlist often depends on whether their families are happy with military life. The military needs high-quality recruits who will stay long enough to make the expense of their recruiting and training worthwhile. Therefore, it must ensure that service members' spouses and children are satisfied enough with military life, despite its many challenges, to encourage and support their service member's decision to join and remain in the military."[14]

There is no question that military families face the possibility that their service members could be risking serious injury or death whether during training, while operating military equipment, or in wartime deployment to combat areas. And any death of a family member or friend (military or citizen) is heartbreaking and often difficult to deal with. But when a family member is in the armed forces, spouses and children face what the U.S. Department of Defense (DOD) calls "catastrophic" stress. "This may be particularly true in the current conflicts,

Military Family Month

In 2016, then-president Barack Obama issued a proclamation, announcing November as Military Family Month. He declared in part,

> For generations, brave Americans have stepped forward and answered our country's call to serve in our Armed Forces. With honor and distinction, our Soldiers, Sailors, Airmen, Marines, and Coast Guardsmen fight to defend the principles upon which our Republic was founded so that we might live in a freer and more prosperous world. Behind these courageous Americans stand spouses, children, and parents who give up precious time with their loved ones, bearing the burden of long deployments and difficult moves, and oftentimes putting their careers on hold. During Military Family Month, we salute the families of those who proudly are a part of our Nation's unbroken chain of patriots for their unwavering devotion, and we renew our sacred vow to uphold our promise to our troops, our veterans, and their families. . . .
>
> We must always be there for our service members and their families—just as they are there for us. Through the thickest of fights and the darkest of nights, our extraordinary military families—our heroes on the home front—stand alongside our patriots in uniform, and in their example we see the very best of our country's spirit. This month, let us thank them for their tremendous devotion to duty and for their unyielding sacrifice. Let us honor their resolve and patriotism and uphold our solemn responsibility to ensure the priorities of our Nation reflect the priorities of our military families.[c]

as the sustained high operational tempo means that families face more frequent, longer, combat deployments with shorter breaks between them." Studies have found that young people ages eleven to seventeen whose parents have been deployed have a higher incidence of emotional problems than the national average in the same age group, the DOD reported.[15]

As former president Barack Obama stressed in his 2016 Presidential Proclamation during Military Family Month, "We must always be there for our service members and their families—just as they are there for us." © iStock.com/spfoto

The National Military Family Association published an article based on surveys over four years of teenagers whose parents were or are in the military. The article points out that the survey "is not a scientific study, but the result of one open-ended question about military life posed to thousands of military youth." Titled "10 Things Military Teens Want You to Know," the article notes that teens are proud of their military parents. But they also "have complicated emotions relating to their military parents' service. Sometimes, for example, they resent parents for missing important events, even while being proud of the work they are doing. Military teens overwhelmingly name their military parent as a positive role model."[16] Teenagers also understand the realities of war and worry about what will happen if a parent is deployed to a combat area.

The article explains that teens "take on a lot of responsibility (but sometimes, it's too much). When military parents go away for deployments or Temporary Duty (TDY), their family responsibilities fall to the caregiver at home. It's common for teens and pre-teens to assume at least some of those responsibilities." Yet they appreciate the fact that in many cases they are able to experience living in diverse places, since families of active duty military personnel have lived in "Germany, Japan, and Italy for several years at a time. Teens and pre-teens may have even picked up a foreign language or two during their mom or dad's tour overseas." In addition, military teens appreciate public recognition of their parents' service.[17]

Facing the Worst Fear

If ever there is a time when military families have to face their worst fears it is learning that a family member in the armed forces has been killed. Since the terrorists' attacks on the United States in 2001, "more than 16,000 uniformed service members have died on active duty," stated a report in *The Future of the Children*. Yet "little empirical research has been done on how a parent's death, especially a parent's death in combat, affects children in the military."[18]

The same issue of *The Future of the Children* pointed out that "military families are a diverse population whose needs vary over time and across demographic groups. No single story can encapsulate who military families are or what they need to flourish in military and civilian communities."[19]

Nevertheless, the *Washington Post* created a website titled Children of the Fallen: Patriots of Loss and recorded how young people have dealt with their military parents' deaths. One example is Jordan Phaneuf, who was only nine years old when her father, Army Staff Sgt. Joseph E. Phaneuf II, was killed by a roadside bomb on December 15, 2006, in the U.S. war in Afghanistan. As a college student in 2015, Jordan recalled that at her father's wake a stranger came over to talk to her. "While holding my hand, he looks at me and tells me how great of a man my father was, how he is such a hero for giving his life," Jordan wrote in an essay for her high school English class. "He tells me how my father didn't just do this for my family, but what my father did was also for him and everyone else in this country." She added that the stranger "was the one who made me realize that my father's death was not just a tragedy, but it turned him into a hero."[20]

Another college student whose military father died is Leah Andrews. Her father, Air Force Master Sgt. Evander Andrews, was killed in Qatar. He was working on an airfield in the early days of the war in 2001 when a forklift crushed and killed him. Years later, as a student at Gardner-Webb University in Boiling Springs, North Carolina, Leah follows a family tradition: she, along with her sisters and mother, set aside the day of her father's death for remembering. She usually wears or carries something that was his, such as his Air Force–issue Randolph Aviator sunglasses that she hooks to her collar.[21]

Twelve other young people—male and female—whose parents were killed while in the armed forces are profiled on the website. You can click on each of their photographs and read their stories. As Steve Hendrix wrote in the introduction, "Those profiled range in age from 6 to 34 and live from Connecticut to California. They are second-graders and high school seniors, athletes and artists, strugglers and strivers, each finding his or her own path through a childhood marred by loss. Each living with a piece of himself or herself forever gone."[22]

VIGILS

"This is not going to be easy. I keep thinking that I am going to see him tomorrow."
—*Brenden Gogan, a senior at Nashua High School North, at a vigil for a lost friend*[1]

Dictionary definitions of *vigil* state that it is "a watch or a period of watchful attention" or "an act or period of watching or surveillance." For many people, vigils mean a gathering to honor the deceased—a family member or close friend, coworker, or classmate—with prayers, flowers, candles, photographs, artwork, and other items. Those who take part in such a vigil, remember the life of the deceased individual, and feel free to display their emotions, ranging from disbelief to anger to grief.

There are also vigils for those in the armed services who have been killed while in combat or on active duty. In addition, U.S. veterans who have died are honored with vigils. These military vigils are patriotic commemorations. American flags are prominently displayed, and armed service members as well as the family of the fallen military are in attendance.

In recent years, however, vigils have taken on a broader meaning. Participants stand watch and hold vigils regarding life-and-death issues such as abortion, climate change, civil/human rights, and illegal immigration to the United States. For example, the *Washington Post* published a feature in 2016 titled "Immigrants and Advocates Hold Vigil Outside Supreme Court." The article described how thousands of families were standing before the U.S. Supreme Court building to await the outcome of arguments over *United States v. Texas*. The case involved former president Barack Obama's executive order to expand the Deferred Action for Childhood Arrivals (DACA) program, which would limit deportation of illegal immigrants and allow them to apply for work permits. The state of Texas challenged the program and the federal court blocked implementation of the DACA. Obviously, the participants at the vigil were disappointed, but vowed to keep advocating for DACA.

Vigils to Mourn and Commemorate the Deceased

Perhaps you have been one of the countless young people who have participated in a vigil to honor or mourn someone who has died. In Jersey City, New Jersey, for example, Lincoln High School teenagers held a vigil in September 2016 for their classmate Anthony Rios. Seventeen-year-old Rios was accidentally shot by the son of a federal police officer, according to a news report. The shooter was charged with "aggravated manslaughter and weapons charges." High school seniors planned the candlelight vigil for Rios and held it near a court where Rios frequently played basketball. The teens at the park vigil "wore shirts with 'Ricoville'—a nickname the teen often went by—ironed onto a T-shirt along with his photo." Some classmates described Rios as a very happy person, and "the senior class president Alondra Collado said to the dozens of people in attendance, 'No one deserves to have their life taken away by a bullet, by violence, by abuse—period.'"[2]

In another candlelight vigil for a teenager in October 2016, friends and family gathered at a bridge in Nashua, New Hampshire, to express their grief and to commemorate Jacob Goulet. Authorities found Goulet's body in the Merrimack River and speculate that during a heavy rainstorm Goulet might have been swept into a sewer drain and drowned.

Still another vigil was observed in October 2016 to commemorate the death of fourteen-year-old Jamarr Mack Jr. of St. Louis, Missouri. He died after he

It is a common practice at vigils for participants to place flowers and candles at the site where a person has died. © iStock.com/TokenPhoto

Gun Violence

Unfortunately, vigils often are held for young people killed by guns. Children and teenagers are killed by guns every single day in the United States. Statistics regarding these deaths are compiled by various organizations and government agencies. One is the Brady Campaign to End Gun Violence, named for Jim Brady, who was seriously injured when he was shot during the assassination attempt on President Ronald Reagan in 1981. Brady and his wife, Sarah, established the campaign to raise awareness about gun violence and to help prevent criminals and other prohibited purchasers (such as mentally disturbed people) from buying guns. To repeat statistics, the Brady website indicates that each year "over 17,000 (17,360) American children and teens are shot in murders, assaults, suicides & suicide attempts, unintentional shootings, or by police intervention." On a daily basis,

- 48 children and teens are shot in murders, assaults, suicides & suicide attempts, unintentional shootings, and police intervention.
- 7 children and teens die from gun violence: 4 are murdered, 2 kill themselves.
- 40 children and teens are shot and survive: 32 shot in an assaults, 1 in a suicide attempt, 8 shot unintentionally.[a]

The Brady Campaign's aim is to cut gun violence in half by 2025.

was fatally shot while walking home from the library. His family contends that Jamarr was killed by another teenager during an argument. CrimeStoppers offered "a reward up to $5,000 for anyone who has information leading to the arrest of the person or persons who killed Mack," according to Fox News2. At the vigil, friends, family, and neighbors lit candles and released balloons in honor of Jamarr. Some wore T-shirts with the words "We Must Stop the Killing."[3]

Mourning Mass Killings

Tragically and historically, mass murders have occurred worldwide for eons. They still happen in current times, and the United States is not exempt from such horrific catastrophes, as anyone who reads or listens to the news knows. One of the worst horrors occurred on September 11, 2001, when terrorists flew planes into the World Trade Center in New York City and the Pentagon outside Washington, DC. One plane crashed in a Pennsylvania field. More than three thousand people were killed in New York and DC.

When mass killings happen, people gather to light candles or take part in vigils to commemorate and mourn those who are murdered. Unfortunately, many vigils for victims of mass murders have been held in the United States. Some examples:

- In Aurora, Colorado, on July 20, 2012, twelve people were shot to death and fifty-eight were wounded in a movie theater. Twenty-four-year-old James E. Holmes was the killer and was arrested outside of the movie theater.
- At the end of 2012, a horrendous mass killing occurred at the Sandy Hook Elementary School in Newtown, Connecticut. Twenty-year-old Adam Lanza gunned down twenty young children and six adults before turning the gun on himself. Before the school murders, he had killed his mother. The Sandy Hook murders are still mourned in vigils marking that tragic day.
- On October 1, 2015, at Umpqua Community College in Roseburg, Oregon, nine people were killed by Christopher Sean Harper-Mercer. He died in a gun battle with police at the college. Hours after the killing, hundreds of the Roseburg community gathered for a candlelight vigil.
- Two months later, on December 2, 2015, in San Bernardino, California, a married couple—Syed Rizwan Farook and Tashfeen Malik—murdered fourteen of their fellow employees at a public health department staff party. The couple were shot dead by police. Hundreds of people gathered on December 3 at the San Bernardino County Board of Supervisors and also at California State University–San Bernardino to hold candlelight vigils and mourn the victims of the shootings. Several days later, thousands attended a vigil at the San Manuel Stadium in San Bernardino.
- In June 2016, numerous vigils involved thousands of people who gathered at memorials that were held nationwide and abroad. They mourned and remembered those killed in what is considered America's worst mass murder since 2001. A heavily armed gunman, Omar Saddiqui Mateen, shot and killed forty-nine people and injured fifty-three in an Orlando, Florida, nightclub called the Pulse, a gay venue. Police shot and killed Mateen. Those who came to a vigil in Orlando lit candles, listened to songs, and flew rainbow flags. In English and Spanish, speakers urged the city to unite and to prevent intimidation of the lesbian, gay, bisexual, and transgender community.

If you or anyone you know has had to cope with the emotional impact of mass murder, some helpful advice comes from organizations like the American Counseling Association (ACA). On its website, the ACA emphasizes the need to first take care of yourself. "Monitor all of your physical health needs—being sure to eat, sleep, exercise, and (if possible) maintain a normal daily routine." Other suggestions, somewhat abbreviated, include the following:

- Pay attention to your emotional health. . . . Know that others are also experiencing emotional reactions and may need your time and patience to put their feelings and thoughts in order.
- Try to recognize when you or those around you may need extra support. It is not uncommon for individuals of all ages to experience stress reactions when exposed (even through media) to shootings or mass violence. . . .
- Avoid overexposure to media. While it is important to stay informed, media portrayals of shootings and mass deaths have been shown to cause acute stress and posttraumatic stress symptoms. Limit your exposure and take a break from news sources.
- Maintain contact with friends and family. These individuals can provide you with emotional support to help deal with difficult times. . . . Maintain practices that you have found to provide emotional relief. Remind yourself of people and events which are meaningful and comforting.
- Talk to others as needed. It is important to ask for help if you are having trouble recovering and everyday tasks seem difficult to manage.[4]

Thanatologists

Among those who attempt to ease the pain and grief occurring after death are thanatologists. They take their name from a Greek term defined as the scientific study of death and its social, psychological, legal, and moral aspects. Their main purpose is to soothe and comfort the dying, sometimes taking part in vigils for terminally ill patients.

Music is one aspect of thanatology. The ancient Greeks, Celts, and medieval monks were among those who used music or chants to help bring about a peaceful death. Today practitioners in this field use the harp, voice, and a special repertoire of music at the bedside of dying patients. Called a music vigil, this service is delivered by one or two highly trained music thanatologists, who serve the needs of the dying and their loved ones with prescriptive music. According to the Music Thanatology Association International, music can help ease pain, agitation, and other physical symptoms. A music vigil also provides a sense of serenity and comfort, soothing the dying and those in attendance.

L. W. Nixon Library
Butler Community College
901 South Haverhill Road
El Dorado, Kansas 67042-3280

While thanatologists may not be called to hold a vigil for young people who are near death, some teens may experience a music vigil while visiting a terminally ill parent or grandparent or elderly friend. Bringing in a thanatologist for a death vigil may take place at home, in a hospice center, hospital, or other healthcare facility.

In recent years, courses in thanatology have become part of some university and college curricula. A series of courses may qualify students to receive an interdisciplinary minor in thanatology. At some universities, a certificate program is available for students preparing for a career in thanatology.

Studies in thanatology may include nearly anything that is related to dying, death, and bereavement. Topics such as aging, AIDS, euthanasia, funerals, palliative care, suicide, and urban violence could be covered. If you have an interest in a possible career in grief counseling, you might want to check out the textbook *Handbook of Thanatology: The Essential Body of Knowledge for the Study of Death,*

"Thanatopsis"

The title of the poem "Thanatopsis" by American William Cullen Bryant (1794–1878) in Greek means "meditation on death," "contemplation of death," or "view of death." Bryant, who much later was called the father of American poetry, wrote the first version of "Thanatopsis" in the autumn of 1811 when he was seventeen years old. He was inspired, some say, by his voracious reading of poetry books in his father's library. Others suggest that because Bryant grew up within view of a rural graveyard, he was inspired to write the poem.

The poem passed through several early drafts, one of which Bryant left on his father's desk. While Bryant was practicing law in Plainfield, Massachusetts, his father recopied the poem and submitted it along with another poem to the *North American Review*, which published "Thanatopsis" anonymously in 1817. This early version included four rhymed stanzas dealing with Bryant's fear and dread of death, which were later removed from the poem. Nevertheless, the poem was a critical success. Bryant reached the peak of his career in the 1830s. His "Thanatopsis" can be found in most representative anthologies of American verse and is available online.

Dying, and Bereavement, edited by David K. Meagher and David E. Balk (2013). *The Last Dance: Encountering Death and Dying* (2011) is a popular publication for a general audience and provides a comprehensive introduction to the main issues in contemporary thanatology. A tenth edition was published in 2014. Other suggested publications include those written by Elizabeth Kübler-Ross, known for her groundbreaking book *On Death and Dying*. It describes how patients deal with death and has been read and studied by countless health-care providers and nursing/counseling students.

An Unending Vigil

Simply mention the Arlington National Cemetery in Arlington, Virginia, and many people recall that it is the site for a never-ending vigil held at the Tomb of the Unknown Soldier. The tomb is a white marble sarcophagus—a stone coffin. The word *sarcophagus* comes from a kind of stone that Greeks believed consumed the flesh of the dead, so it was commonly used for coffins. Compared to such monuments as the Lincoln or Jefferson monuments or the World War II memorial, it is not a huge edifice. It is decorated with Greek neoclassic columns, and on the side facing toward Washington, DC, there are three figures representing Peace, Victory, and Valor. On the back of the tomb, the following words are inscribed: "Here rests in Honored Glory an American Soldier Known but to God."

If you have visited the nation's monuments in Washington and nearby Arlington, you have probably witnessed the vigil at the tomb. Sentinels hold a vigil (stand guard) at the tomb around the clock, 365 days a year, day or night, in any weather. In fact, there has been a sentinel on duty in front of the tomb every minute of every day since 1937.

Sentinels who stand watch at the Tomb of the Unknown Soldier consider it an honored duty. While on guard, the sentinel marches continuously. He holds his weapon on his shoulder, marches twenty-one steps down the mat in front of the tomb, turns, and repeats the process. The number of steps symbolizes the twenty-one-gun salute to honor the military dead. After the turn, the sentinel places his weapon on the shoulder closest to the visitors to signify that he stands between the tomb and any possible threat.

The changing of the guard is an elaborate ritual conducted with solemn precision. From October 1 to March 31, sentinels change every hour on the hour; from April 1 to September 30, when there are numerous visitors to the tomb, the guard changes every half hour. All the sentinels are volunteers of the 3rd U.S. Infantry Regiment headquartered in Fort Myer, Virginia. "Each soldier must be in superb physical condition, possess an unblemished military record and be between 5 feet, 10 inches and 6 feet, 4 inches tall, with a proportionate weight and build," according to the monument's website. Soldiers are interviewed and undergo a two-week trial to determine their capability. The website explains,

> New sentinels learn the history of Arlington National Cemetery and the grave locations of nearly 300 veterans. They learn the guard-change ceremony and the manual of arms that takes place during the inspection portion of the Changing of the Guard. Sentinels learn to keep their uniforms and weapons in immaculate condition.
>
> The sentinels will be tested to earn the privilege of wearing the silver Tomb Guard Identification Badge after several months of serving. First, they are tested on their manual of arms, uniform preparation and their walks. Then, the Badge Test is given. The test is 100 randomly selected questions of the 300 items memorized during training on the history of Arlington National Cemetery and the Tomb of the Unknown Soldier. The would-be badge holder must get more than 95 percent correct to succeed.[5]

At the Tomb of the Unknown Soldier in Arlington National Cemetery, a sentinel stands guard. © iStock.com/jmaehl

Vigils Concerning Life-and-Death Issues

As noted previously, millions of people hold vigils to take a stand and show their support for or opposition to various issues that could determine the life or death of countless individuals. That is, people gather—usually in the streets or in front of public buildings—to express their views with chants, signs, and sometimes physical confrontations regarding issues such as abortion, the death penalty, civil/human rights, illegal immigrants, and peace.

Abortion

For decades, abortion vigils have been highly emotional and sometimes violent, with proponents and opponents congregating in the streets for hours and days at a time. In technical terms, an abortion is an herbal, medical, or surgical procedure to end a pregnancy. Most abortions in the United States occur before viability, or before a fetus is able to survive on its own—between twenty-one and twenty-eight weeks after conception. Deliberately ending a pregnancy is legal in the United States within specified limits, but it is one of the most divisive issues in the nation. It is especially controversial when teenagers opt for abortions, although teen pregnancy and abortion rates have declined, reaching "new historic lows in 2011" (the most recent data), according to the Alan Guttmacher Institute, the leading organization that gathers and analyzes data on abortions.[6]

Abortion issues are usually framed as pro-life or pro-choice. Advocates on the pro-life side believe that when a woman has an abortion a person (child) dies in the process—in other words, they argue that the fetus has a right to life and that deliberately ending a pregnancy is murder. Pro-choice supporters believe a fetus is not yet a person and a woman should have the right to decide what happens to her body. Both sides no doubt will continue to hold vigils on this controversial issue.

Death Penalty

Another type of vigil includes protesters against and supporters of capital punishment—the death penalty. In such cases, two opposing groups may camp outside a penitentiary—one opposed to the death penalty and the other for it. Death penalty opponents often light candles and pray for the prisoner. Death penalty supporters wait for the execution, believing that it is an appropriate punishment for the crime (murder or treason) committed.

Teen Views on the Death Penalty

The Annenberg Classroom, a website for civics education, posts high school social studies questions and discussions. Questions were asked about the death penalty: Should it be carried out or restricted? Is it constitutional or does the practice violate the constitutional right to protection against cruel and unusual punishment?

Students in diverse states posted their comments from 2011 through 2016. On the pro side, junior high school students in Stroudsburg, Pennsylvania, penned their views in March 2016. Gabrielle wrote, "I believe that the death penalty is constitutional, only if someone does something too bad to just put in jail. For instance, if you kill someone for no main purpose, you deserve the death penalty." Emma Scott agreed, writing, "I believe that there should be a death penalty. If someone takes another's life, then they should lose their liberty and life. As long as the person on death row is killed in a humane way, it's constitutional. They should suffer the pain that their victim did." Carlos posted, "The death penalty is constitutional if it is done in a humane way. Nobody should be killed with assault and cruelty. . . . If someone kills somebody else by accident then it shouldn't be applied. It should be allowed in all states." Samuel stated, "The death penalty is constitutional. States should be allowed to carry out executions because people who did serious crimes like mass murder and treason don't deserve to still be allowed to walk around."[b]

Other comments on the website were decidedly against capital punishment, declaring execution immoral, unconstitutional, and inhumane. Some opined that carrying out an execution was the same as committing another murder. Several expressed concerns about the possibility of killing an individual who might later be found innocent.

On another website, Sierra Watts, co-editor of Blue Ridge High School student newspaper in New Milford, Pennsylvania, shared her view about the death penalty in an essay. In no uncertain terms, she began, "The death penalty is one of the worst things that exists in today's society. . . . Why can't we, as human beings, evolve from the medieval idea of retribution. . . . Seeking revenge is not a moral way to seek justice. . . . It is more of a punishment to the offender to be put in jail rather than be killed."[c]

Still one more opinion was expressed by Michael F. of Westwood, Massachusetts, who wrote in an essay for *Teen Ink* that "it seems that our government is being hypocritical when it states that capital punishment is allowable because, after all, the criminal did murder an innocent victim, and therefore should be killed. This is known as the 'eye-for-an-eye, and tooth-for-a-tooth theory.' Of course, if we used this system all the time, there would be no need for laws. If someone hits me, I would hit him/her back . . . we can all be primitive again."[d]

Eighteen states plus the District of Columbia ban the death penalty. The states are Alaska, Connecticut, Hawaii, Illinois, Iowa, Maine, Maryland, Massachusetts, Michigan, Minnesota, Nebraska, New Jersey, New Mexico, New York, North Dakota, Rhode Island, Vermont, West Virginia, and Wisconsin, according to ProCon.org, which explores controversial issues.[7]

Although most vigils for or against the death penalty primarily include adult participants, young people have definite views about this punishment. They express their objections or support on various websites or in print materials.

Civil Rights/Human Rights Vigils

Civil rights or human rights vigils are perhaps some of the most widespread and consistent in the United States. Participants in these vigils stand against discrimination and promote cultural diversity and harmony. For example, in Pennsylvania, students at Penn State York in West Chester held a candlelight vigil on October 6, 2016, led by then sophomore Alyssa Zelwalk. She noted,

It is important now more than ever that we join together, as compassionate human beings, rather than let [terrorists] events tear us apart and define who we are and how society will treat each other moving forward. . . . It is also vitally important that we do not live our lives in fear, because when we live in fear, we're not really living. Recent events have reminded us that it's important to love, to live, to be compassionate, and to hug the ones we love just a little bit harder every day.[8]

One of the students, Samantha Jeune, "read a poem that she wrote about her struggles with racial issues" and spoke of "the difficulties she has faced on campus when it comes to acceptance." In Jeune's words, "After my first semester, I felt like I didn't belong, and there were multiple instances where I wanted to transfer out. But I was able to get support systems through family, friends and professors on campus who cared about me, and that encouraged me to stay. . . . But not everyone gets that experience, and not everyone stays. I think it says a lot about our campus climate. . . . We have issues of racism, sexism, xenophobia and homophobia on our campus, and that needs to be acknowledged."[9]

One of the largest ever human rights vigils in the United States was held the day after the inauguration of Donald J. Trump as the forty-fifth president of the United States. Millions assembled in Washington, DC, to take part in a peaceful but highly vocal vigil called the Women's March, held on January 21, 2017. The gathering took place to show support for women's rights and to protest the election of Trump. Similar peaceful gatherings occurred in cities all across the United States. Political vigils against the president's policies and executive orders have continued, particularly when Trump banned refugees and visa holders from Muslim countries from entering the United States. Protesters again gathered in major cities across the nation and even in smaller towns. Vigils like these are expected to continue.

On the other hand, millions of participants have held political gatherings before and after Trump's inauguration to support his "Make America Great Again" policies. Supporters, many of them adamant, stand up for Trump's executive order to round up and deport immigrants who have illegally entered the United States. Vigils are also held to show support for Trump's economic, education, and health-care views, as well as his pledge to reduce regulations on businesses.

Peace Vigils

The major focus of peace vigils is usually to protest wars. In some cities, peace vigils occur annually, monthly, or on a selected day each week. For instance, just before the Thanksgiving holiday in 2015, students at Penn State York (PSY) held a Vigil for Peace on the front steps of Sykes Student Union. The vigil was prompted by the multiple terrorist attacks in Paris on November 13 that killed 130 people, one of them an American—23-year-old Nohemi Gonzalez, an exchange student from Cal State. The PSY students also wanted to draw attention to global disasters and offer hope. Students, faculty, and staff "wrote messages of support for the victims of the terrorist attacks, which were then placed on a display board: 'May you find peace.' . . . 'None of them will be forgotten if they are carried in our hearts,' 'Peace comes after disaster,' and 'Nakupenda,' which means 'I love you' in Swahili, were just a few of the messages left at the site."[10]

In June 2016, dozens of young people and adults gathered at the American Legion Memorial Civic Center in Morton Grove, Illinois, a Chicago suburb, to participate in an interfaith vigil advocating for peace. "Students from the Muslim Community Center Academy performed two songs: Salamun Salam, which translates to 'peaceful peace,' and the Christian melody, *Dona Nobis Pacem*, whose title means 'grant us peace,'" the *Chicago Tribune* reported. Along with the songs, there was a "presentation of pictures and messages written by students at Gemini Junior High School in Niles about what peace means to them."[11]

A group of boys in Bedford, Virginia, held a peace vigil in July 2016 at the local farmer's market. The group known as Boys with a Dream range in age from twelve to sixteen, and most of them have played basketball together. Sixteen-year-old Ta'Ron Robinson organized the group because he wanted to do something for his community, particularly to hold a vigil against hate and violence. Robinson told a reporter for Channel 13 (WSET) that the Prayers for Peace Vigil was an attempt "to help everyone come together and pray" so that their community would not experience the kind of violence like the 2016 nightclub killings in Orlando, Florida.[12] They also held a prayer vigil for peace after five police officers in Dallas, Texas, were killed in August 2016.

Bedford County sheriff Mike Brown was so impressed with the boys' efforts that he and the Virginia Sheriff's Association and the National Sheriff's Association presented a gift to the boys: an all-expenses-paid visit to a Washington Nationals baseball game and a tour of the U.S. Capitol in September 2016. At the time, Robinson again spoke with WSET, saying, "A lot of evil is going on around the world and I think we are finally trying to make a change. I think everyone is going to hop on and help us make the change." Another member chimed in to say the group could help a lot of kids stay out of trouble. Sheriff Brown praised the group. "It took courage to do what they are doing," he told WSET.[13]

LIVING WITH DEADLY DISEASES

···

"I'm not giving up hope for one second, no matter what the doctors say."
—teenager Chris Togneri, who was dying of cancer[1]

Decades ago, the deadly viruses smallpox and influenza (flu) killed thousands in the United States. But today vaccinations and antivirus drugs for flu and other deadly diseases are now available for Americans. However, many people in the United States still face terminal illnesses, such as heart disease, cancer, HIV/ AIDS, and other viral diseases. Teens and young adults are among the victims.

Cancer and Young Adults

One of the most feared diseases is cancer. Nearly 585,000 Americans died of cancer in 2013. It is the second leading cause of death in the United States (heart disease heads the list). "About 70,000 young people (ages 15–39) are diagnosed with cancer each year in the United States," the National Cancer Institute reports, adding,

> Young adults are more likely than either younger children or older adults to be diagnosed with certain cancers, such as Hodgkin's lymphoma, melanoma, testicular cancer, thyroid cancer, and sarcomas. However, the incidence of specific cancer types varies according to age. Leukemia, lymphoma, testicular cancer, and thyroid cancer are the most common cancers among 15–24-year-olds. Among 25–39-year-olds, breast cancer and melanoma are the most common.[2]

One teenager, Casandra Callender of Windsor Locks, Connecticut, was diagnosed with Hodgkin's lymphoma, a cancer of the lymphatic system. Casandra,

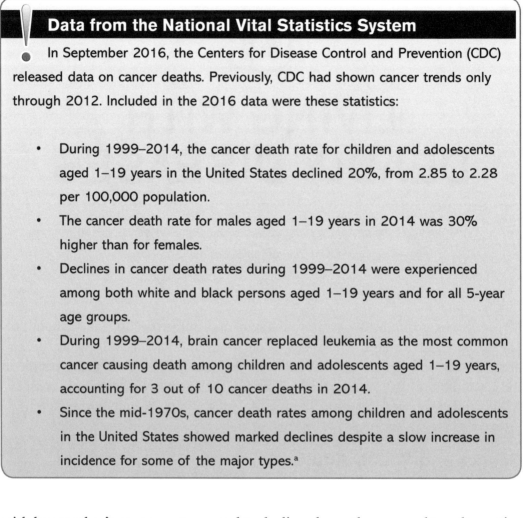

Data from the National Vital Statistics System

In September 2016, the Centers for Disease Control and Prevention (CDC) released data on cancer deaths. Previously, CDC had shown cancer trends only through 2012. Included in the 2016 data were these statistics:

- During 1999–2014, the cancer death rate for children and adolescents aged 1–19 years in the United States declined 20%, from 2.85 to 2.28 per 100,000 population.
- The cancer death rate for males aged 1–19 years in 2014 was 30% higher than for females.
- Declines in cancer death rates during 1999–2014 were experienced among both white and black persons aged 1–19 years and for all 5-year age groups.
- During 1999–2014, brain cancer replaced leukemia as the most common cancer causing death among children and adolescents aged 1–19 years, accounting for 3 out of 10 cancer deaths in 2014.
- Since the mid-1970s, cancer death rates among children and adolescents in the United States showed marked declines despite a slow increase in incidence for some of the major types.[a]

with her mother's agreement, wanted to decline chemotherapy and try alternative treatments, but in 2015 Casandra was seventeen years old. She was a minor and not allowed the make that decision. "The state Department of Children and Families stepped in and a Juvenile Court judge removed her from her home, placed her under guard in the Connecticut Children's Medical Center and ordered her to undergo chemo," according to an NBC news report. "Doctors have said her odds at recovery are 80 to 85 percent with chemo, but that she will die without it."[3]

After five months of treatment, she was released from the hospital. Her cancer was in remission, but in 2016 a malignant mass was found in her lungs. Since by then she had turned eighteen, she was able to make her own decisions and she opted for alternative treatment—some type of holistic medicine. She did not specify what the treatment would be, and at the time there was no prognosis about her chances for survival.

Luke Blanock of Canonsburg, Pennsylvania, was also living with cancer—terminal cancer. A high school athlete, he was diagnosed with Ewing's sarcoma,

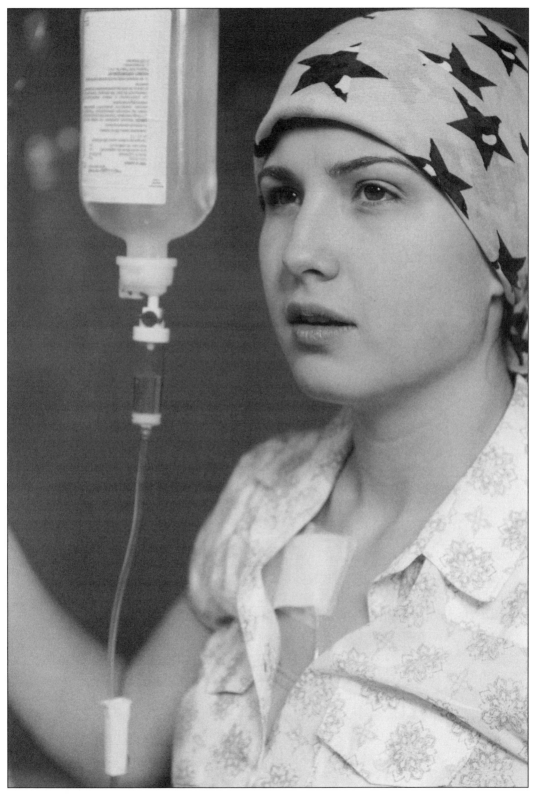

When someone is diagnosed with cancer, chemotherapy is the common treatment. ©
iStock.com/KatarzynaBialasiewicz

a rare bone cancer, in 2013. A high school athlete, he underwent several years of treatment—many rounds of chemotherapy, radiation, and two surgeries. Blanock's cancer went into remission and then spread, but that did not prevent him from living as full a life as possible, reportedly selfless, always smiling, and not showing pain. He graduated from high school, and he and his high school sweetheart, Natalie Britvich, planned to marry. Luke reportedly told Natalie, "I'm not marrying you just to make you a widow. I'm not giving up hope for one second, no matter what the doctors say. I'm going to fight."[4]

When nineteen-year-old Blanock learned that his cancer was terminal, he and Natalie decided they should wed as soon as possible. Luke proposed to Natalie and she readily agreed. With the help of community donations and support through Luke Strong, which funded their wedding, they married in February 2016.

News Channel 11 followed Blanock through his three-year ordeal and reported, "During one of his last interviews with Channel 11, Blanock said he chose to live even when doctors said he was dying. Despite not being able to walk very well, he walked down the aisle to marry his true love, he walked to get his diploma with his class on graduation day, and [on August 6] he was still smiling in his hospital bed, remaining 'Luke Strong' until the very end." He died on August 7, 2016.[5]

British teenager Max Edwards was sixteen years old in 2015 when he was diagnosed with terminal cancer. His story appeared in the *Guardian*, a British newspaper, and was later posted on Pinterest and other websites. Max wrote, "In the past, I have imagined terminal illness as the short and depressing period before a person's premature death, but it somehow doesn't feel nearly as dramatic or upsetting." Max continued to explain that it was difficult to tell friends and family because they would "break down in tears, [and] made the experience not so much sad as really quite awkward." He added,

> This isn't to say that it hasn't been an intense few months, but I can't say that this experience has truly changed me as a person. People have told me how well I'm coping and how they couldn't have done the same in this situation, as though I've faced an unimaginably horrendous set of circumstances and managed to do the impossible (remain positive), but I don't see it that way . . . dying of cancer, in my experience, has been a succession of hospital visits, a lot of pills, and one or two pieces of bad news. But after that, there is an inevitable return to the way you were previously living. Pretty soon I came to realise that it doesn't make any difference if you'll be dead in 10 years or two months; you still get up, have a shower and make a cup of tea.[6]

His lengthy essay ends with this: "While my life may be all I know, I'm nothing more than a dot on this planet. When you take into account the dozens of people I know, the billions I don't, the thousands of miles that separate us, and the ever running river of time on which we all finitely float, you may come to the inevitable and strangely comforting realisation that we are all going to die: me, you and everyone else. Get over it."[7] A week after he wrote his essay, Max Edwards died.

Read or Watch It

The novel *Me and Earl and the Dying Girl* by Jesse Andrews (2012) is a sad but not a maudlin story. It is even humorous at times and often bawdy. A film by the same name and script written by Andrews was released in 2015.

In the story, Greg is a sarcastic high school senior who is friendly but standoffish because he is insecure and does not want to be criticized or judged. His family includes his mom, Marla; his father, Victor, who is a professor of classics; and two sisters. His only friend is Earl Jackson who comes from a home with a drug-addicted single mother and numerous step siblings. Earl is an irreverent, foulmouthed teen and spends a lot of hours in the Gaines's home.

Greg and Earl are movie buffs and also have a near-obsessive hobby making offbeat movies. Their moviemaking is interrupted when Greg is pressured by his mother to visit a one-time classmate, Rachel Kushner, who has acute myelogenous leukemia, a cancer of the blood and bone marrow.

Rachel and Greg were once classmates in sixth grade while in Hebrew school, but since then have had little contact. Reluctantly Greg visits Rachel and at first they have awkward conversations. But in later visits Greg attempts to bring Rachel a little cheer, mimicking film actors. When Rachel suggests that he should make his own films, Greg admits that he and his friend, Earl, are already doing that. But he explains that the movies just are not good enough to show anyone. Greg and Earl decide to make a video about Rachel as a way to show they care about her and her life. But they don't want anyone to know about it.

The filmmaking process is haphazard and comical as the boys make a documentary of Rachel's life. No one is allowed to see their effort. But Greg's mother manages to find a copy of *Rachel, the Film* and she and Rachel's mother convince the high school principal to show the movie to the entire school. At the time, Rachel is in the hospital for chemotherapy.

After Rachel returns home, her cancer spreads. Greg meanwhile learns that Earl gave Rachel their experimental film to watch and races to Earl's house in a rage. Earl angrily tells Greg that Rachel deserves to see the film, especially since she is close to death.

The ending is sad, but not unbearably so. Greg mourns Rachel's death as do all the other main characters in the story. You have to read it or watch the movie to decide for yourself what you think about death, Greg and Earl, and the dying girl.

When Deadly Influenza (Flu) Strikes

History lessons and textbooks often include discussions of the flu pandemic of 1918 and 1919 that killed tens of millions worldwide. "Among them were 675,000 Americans."[8] Although flu vaccinations and antibiotics for bacterial infections help prevent flu deaths today, widespread outbreaks of this infectious disease have killed thousands of people in modern times. "The flu pandemic of 2009–10 killed 18,449 people around the world," noted Richard Knox on NPR (National Public Radio).[9] The virus was and is called H1N1 type A influenza, which was nicknamed swine flu, because it was transmitted originally from live pigs, although that is no longer the case. "People get the disease from other people, not from pigs," notes WebMD.[10]

In 2013, flu outbreaks were reported in numerous states. In Minnesota, for example, the health department reported that five hundred people were hospitalized with flu and five died. One of the victims was a physically fit and active fourteen-year-old, Carly Christenson, of St. Louis Park. She had had a flu shot and before being infected was a healthy teenager. Carly was on the junior varsity basketball team at St. Louis Park High School. When she became infected, she was hospitalized and died of influenza complications on January 8, 2013.

One of Carly's classmates, Gabrielle, wrote on the YouTube remembrance site, "I miss [Carly] so much. She was one of my friends. Rest in paradise Carly." Adam wrote, "She still comes up in my thoughts every single day." Doug had this to say, "I mourn the loss of a beautiful young lady. I didn't know Carly personally, but her life touched others I care about deeply." And Haley wrote on the site, "i miss carly so much. cant believe shes gone."[11]

In 2015, a major flu outbreak occurred in Iowa, where health officials predicted that one thousand Iowans would die from the virus, according to a report on WHO TV. A healthy and active Iowa teenager, fourteen-year-old Amber Gray, contracted the virus. She was hospitalized with a dangerously high temperature in late December 2015 and died days later "from pneumonia and sepsis [blood infection]," which are complications of influenza, the TV station reported.[12]

There are no indications that contagious influenza will disappear. It is one of the deadliest viruses. In 2016, *Live Science* reported, "During a typical flu season, up to 500,000 people worldwide will die from the illness. . . . But occasionally, when a new flu strain emerges, a pandemic results with a faster spread of disease and, often, higher mortality rates."[13]

HIV/AIDS

The disease known as human immunodeficiency virus (HIV), which leads to acquired immune deficiency disorder, or AIDS, has had a significant impact on world health and on Americans since the first cases were diagnosed in 1981. In one of the most publicized U.S. cases, Ryan White became infected with AIDS in the early 1980s and was often bullied as a result. He noted, "Because of the lack of education on AIDS, discrimination, fear, panic, and lies surrounded me."[14]

AIDS became a global epidemic. However, in the United States, access to health care and to medicines have helped slow its progress. The death rate and the rate of cases that progress from HIV, the virus that leads to AIDS, has slowed since 1995.

According to the CDC,

- An estimated 9,731 youth aged 13 to 24 were diagnosed with HIV in 2014 in the United States. Eighty-one percent (7,868) of diagnoses among youth occurred in persons aged 20 to 24.
- Among youth aged 13 to 24 diagnosed with HIV in 2014, 80% (7,828) were gay and bisexual males. Of those newly diagnosed young gay and bisexual males, 55% (4,321) were black, 23% (1,786) were Hispanic/Latino, and 16% (1,291) were white.
- From 2005 to 2014, HIV diagnoses among both black and Hispanic/Latino gay and bisexual men aged 13 to 24 increased about 87%. Among young white gay and bisexual men, HIV diagnoses increased 56%. However, the most recent 5 years of data (2010–2014) indicate that the diagnoses among black and white gay and bisexual men aged 13 to 24 have stabilized and the increase has slowed to 16% among Hispanic/Latinos.
- In 2014, an estimated 1,716 youth aged 13 to 24 were diagnosed with AIDS, representing 8% of total AIDS diagnoses that year.[15]

It Happened to Ryan White

Ryan White's story about his HIV infection has been remembered long after the eighteen-year-old's death in 1990. Ryan, who lived with his mother and siblings in Indiana, was infected with HIV when he had a blood transfusion as a child. He needed the transfusion for hemophilia, a disorder that prevents blood from clotting. Ryan was diagnosed with HIV in 1984.

On April 8, 2016, a program in memory of Ryan's death aired on *PBS NewsHour*. *Remembering Ryan White, the Teen Who Fought the Stigma of Aids*, by Professor Howard Markel, explained that after Ryan's first bout of illness, he

wanted to return to the Western Middle School in Russiaville, Indiana. Sadly, the superintendent of the Western School Corporation (which included his town of Kokomo, Indiana) would not let him return and Ryan was forced to listen in on his seventh grade classes via the telephone. Several school officials, teachers, parents and students erroneously (and cruelly) insisted that Ryan might transmit his HIV by casual contact, such as a handshake, from using the public restrooms or even from handling the newspapers Ryan delivered on his paper route.

It took a court case to allow Ryan to return to his classes, but he was bullied and shunned by other students. The Whites' home was vandalized and at stores "cashiers refused to touch his mother's hands when making change. . . . Not everyone in Kokomo was so vituperative, of course, and there were many families who supported Ryan's desire to attend school." But the Whites decided to move to Cicero, Indiana, where Ryan attended Hamilton Heights High School and was welcomed by the principal and most students.[b]

In 1989, a TV film *The Ryan White Story* was shown nationally, creating widespread public interest and celebrity status for Ryan. Stars like Elton John, Michael Jackson, and Charlie Sheen praised Ryan and his stand to remove the stigma of HIV/AIDS. By early 1990, however, Ryan had difficulty breathing. In March 1990, his condition worsened and he was admitted to Riley Children's Hospital in Indianapolis, Indiana. He died on April 6, 1990.

In August 1990, the Ryan White HIV/AIDS Program was passed. It is the "largest federal program focused specifically on providing HIV care and treatment services to people living with HIV. Working with cities, states, and local community-based organizations, the program provides a comprehensive system of care for people living with HIV who are uninsured or underinsured. A smaller but critical portion of the program is used to fund technical assistance, clinical training, and the development of innovative models of care." The act has been amended and reauthorized four times "to accommodate new and emerging needs, such as an increased emphasis on funding core medical services and changes in funding formulas." The act is available online.[c]

HIV/AIDS increasingly affects women. This is of particular concern because children with AIDS or HIV receive the virus from their mothers. One of those children is Mina, who at the age of fifteen, posted her story on Positive Women's Network. She wrote,

I'm a teenager and I'm in middle school. I'm adopted and I have a big family. I'm HIV positive. I'm the only one of my family members that has HIV. My brothers and sister didn't get it when they were born because only some babies born to a mom with HIV actually get HIV. I am one of the ones that did. I'm just like any other middle schooler that you could ever think of except I just have one difference—HIV. Nobody can see it; it doesn't show. I have to tell them.[16]

Mina wanted to speak out because she didn't like "being hurt by the things people do to us or say" about being HIV positive. She especially dislikes those who say she's "infected" although she knows very well that she has an infectious virus. She explained, "Something that is called 'infected' sounds really disgusting, and gross. I have HIV, and I know for sure that I am NOT disgusting or gross." She added, "I'm a girl, not an infection" and pointed out that

a lot of people panic over HIV, but it's not the worst thing in the whole entire world. I've been taking my meds since I was young and I feel healthy. I feel like any regular teen. . . . If you're wondering if it's troublesome for me to have HIV, it's not. Listen, please: other people who have HIV—especially someone who just got it, because they might be panicking. Listen, young people, older people, teenagers, kids, whoever. It's going to be okay. If you take your meds properly—even if you have to take it every single day of your life—at least it's keeping you healthy. At least you can keep living your life and doing stuff like every other person, just with meds.[17]

Another teenager with HIV, Paige Rawl, told her story to *USA Today* in 2013 when she was eighteen. Paige, of Indianapolis, Indiana, was born with HIV and did not learn she had the virus until she was in fifth grade. While in sixth grade, she confided to a friend that she was HIV positive, and "it took only two weeks for the whole school to find out," according to journalist Clara Ritger. From then on classmates ridiculed and bullied her, calling her PAID, "leaving notes on her locker that read, 'No AIDS at this school.'" She lived in constant fear of other taunts, and her mental stress resulted in seizures and multiple hospital visits. Journalist Ritger wrote, "Paige withdrew from Westlane Middle School. She was home-schooled for the remainder of eighth grade. At Westlane, she was a cheerleader, competed in show choir and played softball and soccer. At home, she was bored."[18]

Paige took up public speaking, which at first was her way of sharing her story to try to reduce the stigma associated with HIV and AIDS. Then it became her way to cope. "The first time I spoke, it was this huge relief," she said. "I was scared and I read off this little piece of paper, but a big, huge weight was lifted off my shoulders."[19]

After her initial experience with speaking out, she has continued her advocacy to reduce the stigma for young people with HIV. Paige takes medication that suppresses the HIV. In 2015, at the age of twenty, she told her story on GirlsHealth.gov, explaining how to live a positive life with HIV, debunking the myths about the virus, and giving advice to young people living with HIV:

Being HIV-positive is nothing to be ashamed of. The disease does not define you as a person. Being HIV-positive is no different than living with any other disease or chronic illness. The most important thing is to create awareness about HIV/AIDS. Educating people about the disease helps reduce the stigma. Also, talking with or meeting other people who are HIV-positive can really help. The moment I got involved with Camp Kindle, a camp for kids and teens infected or affected by HIV/AIDS, I knew that I was not alone. I was able to talk and connect with others who knew exactly what I was going through.[20]

Helpful Organizations

Numerous state, national, and international organizations are available to offer help, advice, and support for people with HIV/AIDS. These include the following:

About HIV

HIV is a disease that kills by weakening the human immune system so that it is vulnerable to attack by other diseases and infections. It can take ten years or more for HIV to develop into AIDS, which is the final stage of HIV infection.

The HIV virus can be transmitted in several ways. It can be spread through sexual intercourse with an infected person or by coming into direct contact with blood from an HIV-infected person (often by sharing contaminated needles used for intravenous injections), or an HIV-positive mother can pass it on to her child before or during birth or through breast-feeding. No evidence has yet shown that HIV can be spread by casual contact such as kissing or hugging, or by sharing dishes or bathrooms.

In most cases, symptoms of HIV are mild and flulike at first, consisting of fever, rash, headache, sore lymph nodes, and general ill health. As the disease progresses, symptoms such as weight loss, fatigue, diarrhea, and various fungal infections may appear. Tuberculosis, cancers, and neurological disorders mark the later stages of the disease. While there is no cure or vaccine for AIDS, there are now drugs and treatments that suppress the HIV virus and fight the secondary infections that come with the disease.

Because the first cases of AIDS in the United States were sexually transmitted or often happened to drug users sharing needles, a stigma has been attached to having the disease. Many groups and organizations have worked hard to educate the public and raise awareness of HIV/AIDS as a disease whose victims deserve compassion and medical treatment.

Until a cure for AIDS is found, research continues while public health officials focus on preventive measures for the disease. These include programs promoting safe sex (using condoms; encouraging sexual abstinence or monogamy) and discouraging risky practices such as sharing or reusing hypodermic needles. Educating the public about the facts of HIV and AIDS is also a high priority of both government and grassroots organizations.

- The Ryan White HIV/AIDS Program (http://hab.hrsa.gov/about-ryan
-white-hivaids-program/about-ryan-white-hivaids-program) says it "provides a comprehensive system of care that includes primary medical care
and essential support services for people living with HIV who are uninsured or underinsured. The Program works with cities, states, and local
community-based organizations to provide HIV care and treatment services to more than half a million people each year."
- The Body has a website (http://www.thebody.com/index/hotlines/other
.html) that lists U.S. HIV/AIDS organizations by state, from Alabama to
Wyoming. Clicking on a state reveals helpful services available. For example, Arizona has eight service centers such as the Southern Arizona AIDS
Foundation, which offers counseling, housing, and nutritional support
for HIV-positive people. California has so many organizations that they
are listed by northern and southern areas as well as by city. In Colorado,
seven organizations are listed; one is the Boulder County AIDS Project,
which provides support, advocacy, and education for HIV-infected and
HIV-affected persons and serves as an outreach and information center to
prevent HIV transmission. Florida, Illinois, Pennsylvania, and New York
also have extensive lists.
- JSI Research and Training Institute, Inc. (named for the founder, John
Snow, Inc.) is a nonprofit "health care consulting and research organization dedicated to improving the health of individuals and communities in
the United States and around the world," according to its website (https://
www.whatworksinyouthhiv.org/who-we-are). "JSI has been committed to
the prevention and treatment of HIV since the beginning of the epidemic,
working with organizations to develop, implement, and evaluate HIV prevention programs and improve HIV health service delivery for people living with HIV. . . . Headquartered in Boston, JSI has seven other domestic
offices and works in 53 countries outside of the U.S."[21]

In addition to the many organizations that offer HIV/AIDS services, there
are numerous annual HIV/AIDS Awareness Days and an HIV Vaccine Awareness Day. The specific days for these events are posted on https://www.aids.gov/
news-and-events/awareness-days/. World AIDS Day is held on the first day of
December each year when people worldwide show their support—often wearing
a symbolic red ribbon—for people living with HIV and to commemorate those
who have died.

END-OF-LIFE DECISIONS AND CARE

"I was like, 'I'm going to be able to walk, I'm going to be with God, I'm going to be free."—fourteen-year-old Jerika Bolen after deciding to remove her ventilator and end her life[1]

Currently there is a national effort to have end-of-life discussions with young seriously ill patients before they are unable to participate and express their wishes. Anyone under the age of eighteen is not legally allowed to make such decisions, but doctors can ask parents to make advanced-care choices for their children. Health-care providers can talk to teenagers and young adults directly, asking them about their end-of-life decisions, but parents retain legal authority over minors. Numerous organizations and medical offices have forms that you can complete to describe who should make medical decisions for you, the types of life support you do or do not want, your spiritual thoughts, and how you wish to be remembered.

Teenager AshLeigh McHale created written directions and made her own decisions about her death. She had been diagnosed with melanoma and the cancer was spreading. In 2014, at the age of seventeen, she and her mother flew from her hometown in Oklahoma to the National Institutes of Health in Bethesda, Maryland, hoping for a cure. But there was little chance. When a social worker asked AshLeigh questions about her preferences for her final days, the teenager wrote down her directives. "When she died in July [2015], she was at home as she had requested," according to a blog post by Jan Hoffman published in the *New York Times*. "Per her instructions, she was laid out for the funeral in her favorite jeans, cowgirl boots and the white shirt she had gotten for Christmas. Later, the family dined, as AshLeigh had directed, on steak fajitas and corn on the cob."[2]

Although the family was in deep mourning, AshLeigh's mother told the reporter, "I don't know what I would have done if I'd had to make these decisions during our extreme grief. . . . But she did it all for me. Even though she got to where she couldn't speak, AshLeigh had her say."[3]

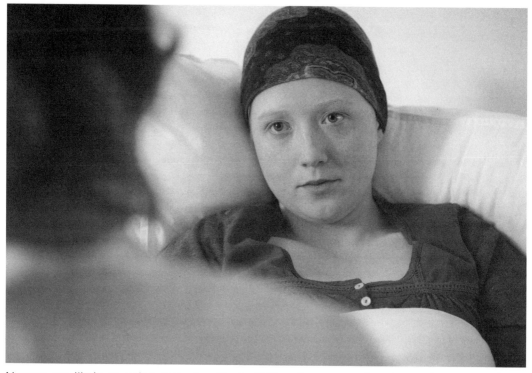

Nurses are likely to ask terminal patients if they have completed an advance directive, a form that spells out their wishes regarding end-of-life care. © *iStock.com/Katarzyna Bialasiewicz*

It Happened to Maggie Worthen

Maggie Worthen, a Smith College student, was close to being pronounced brain dead after she had a stroke in May 2006. A major *Newsweek* feature in 2016 focused on people who have come back from what medical experts diagnose as being in a persistent vegetative state—that is, brain dead. Reporter Aimee Swartz reported,

A CT scan revealed that the stroke in the otherwise healthy 22-year-old was brought on by a blood clot in the basilar artery, a critical blood vessel in the back of her head that supplies oxygen-rich blood to the brainstem, the part of the brain that controls the body's basic life support system. It took 12 hours before neurosurgeons . . . were able to remove the clot and restore blood flow to Maggie's brain. She was in a deep coma, kept alive by the ventilator that told her lungs to breathe.

Maggie was not expected to survive. Doctors advised removing life support, and Worthen's mother was asked for consent to transplant Maggie's organs.

Two weeks later, Maggie was "able to breathe on her own. And after another two weeks, she was strong enough to be transferred to a brain rehabilitation facility. With a tracheostomy helping to keep her airway clear and a feeding tube in place, Maggie received intensive physical, speech and occupational therapy each day." However, "she failed to show any outward signs of progress two months later, [and] was labeled 'vegetative,' a diagnosis that disqualified her from insurance coverage for future rehabilitation."

Worthen was then "transferred to a local nursing home." After a time, she began to react to her mother's and boyfriend's comments. But the medical staff did not believe that Maggie was responding. One physician who questioned whether Maggie was actually in a vegetative state "arranged for her to be transported to Weill Cornell Medical College in New York City. There, she was enrolled in a clinical trial aimed at understanding how the severely injured brain recovers," according to *Newsweek*. When she clearly responded to questions with eye movements, she received more rehabilitation and a medically assisted device to help her communicate. But, sadly, she died of pneumonia in August 2015.

Newsweek reporter Swartz noted that patients who have serious brain injuries are often misdiagnosed and do not receive the care that could help them recover. Dr. Joseph Fins, chief of the division of medical ethics at Weill, told Swartz that "research suggests 68 percent of severely brain-injured patients who receive rehabilitation eventually regain consciousness and that 21 percent of those are able to one day live on their own."[a]

End-of-Life Issues

In the United States and other industrialized nations, people who have terminal illnesses and their families may face end-of-life issues and decisions that can be simple or complex, depending on various factors. There may be issues such as whether a dying person should be cared for at home or in a hospice facility, nursing home, or hospital. Determining whether funds are available for part-time or round-the-clock caregivers is a practical consideration. Legal matters may have to be considered—writing or rewriting a will and advance directives. In some cases, dying patients want to plan their own funerals or make arrangements with a mortuary or funeral home.

Cultural beliefs about preparations for death may be an important matter. Certain rites may be required to be ready for an afterlife, for example. Some cultures forbid speaking about death because of the belief that it will hasten the demise of a patient or will cause unnecessary sadness among relatives. Culture also plays a role in such end-of-life decisions as whether to discontinue the use of life-support systems—some groups want aggressive care, while others do not want suffering prolonged.

Those who favor the concept of being able to manage one's own death believe that quality of life should determine whether a person chooses to die. They measure quality of life in various ways. For example, a person may decide after repeated surgeries and chemotherapy for cancer that quality of life means living the rest of one's days without further invasive medical treatments, even if that hurries death. Or a patient might hasten death if qualities of life such as being able to interact with others or being able to live with dignity are gone. In addition, making decisions about one's own death may be based on the belief that human life cannot be equated with mere biological existence. Simply being alive is not the same as having a life. In other words, life ends when an individual is no longer able to function as a person.

On the other side of this argument are people who adamantly oppose using quality of life as a criterion for decisions on death and dying. They claim that decisions on quality of life will open up the possibility of abuse: poor and vulnerable people, such as the frail elderly, insane, handicapped, and mentally ill or challenged, will be expendable because they are considered a burden to society.

The American Psychological Association argues that more research is needed on how health-care providers can communicate with the dying and understand cultural differences in regard to dying and death. Cultural and socioeconomic differences also need to be addressed.

Only in recent years have end-of-life issues become important topics of discussion in the U.S. general public and among health-care professionals. That is due primarily to medical technology, which has made it possible to effectively treat injury and disease and extend life. Today, it is possible to live several years before succumbing to a terminal illness, but at some point patients or their families may have to make difficult choices about whether to prolong the dying process.

A number of studies have concluded that major end-of-life issues for most people include whether dying will be excruciating and costly and whether health-care personnel will heed individuals' wishes regarding how they want to spend

It Happened to Jerika Bolen

Fourteen-year-old Jerika Bolen of Appleton, Wisconsin, held a prom, which she called her last dance, before she died from a hereditary disease called spinal muscular atrophy type II. The disease is incurable and progressive. It destroys nerve cells in the brain stem and spinal cord, and the muscles deteriorate.

Jerika survived longer than most young people with the illness. For most of her life she was confined to a wheelchair, and by her teen years she could not move most parts of her body, except for her hands and parts of her face. Jerika had several surgeries and had to use a ventilator to breathe. She was in constant pain.

In July 2016, Jerika explained to a reporter for Appleton's *Post-Crescent* why she and her mother, Jen Bolen, planned the prom. "I don't have many friends . . . because I couldn't get out really and do many things because I was in so much pain, and this prom is, we'll, we call it my last dance." When she posted her intent for the prom on Facebook, she was "inundated with friend requests." She attended the prom in a full-length dress and wore her favorite jewelry and purple hair color. The prom was open to the public and more than one thousand people joined her last dance.[b]

In August 2016, Jerika entered a hospice facility with the intention of removing her ventilator. Many times she and her mother, a nurse, had discussed the choice. There were no options left to help Jerika. Removing the ventilator would end her life.

When the last dance was publicized, numerous disability groups attempted to intervene, trying to convince Jerika to reconsider her decision to die. But Jen Bolen said about her daughter, "Any real parent who's seen the suffering she's had would be making this same decision—would let her make this decision."[c] On September 22, 2016, Jerika died. Her mother had this to say: "My only words to anyone questioning this is that I love that girl with every cell in my being . . . and no one in their right mind would let someone suffer like she was."[d]

their last days. In other words, they hope to have a "good death"—dying quickly and painlessly while taking part in an enjoyable activity.

Dignified Death

The concept of dying with dignity is often associated with Death-with-Dignity Acts—state euthanasia laws. But dying with dignity is also a term used to describe death that occurs as a natural process with pain and emotional distress alleviated as opposed to death determined by medical technology that artificially prolongs life. The Free Dictionary defines it this way: "Death that is allowed to occur in accordance with the wishes of a patient. An individual may choose to withdraw from chronic medical therapies, as when there is little expectation of cure. Patients who choose death rather than active treatment often have advanced malignancies, poor performance status, major depression, poor social support, or a desire for a palliative approach to end-of-life care."[4]

In many cases, however, dying is not as easy or peaceful as some imagine, and many individuals die painfully in health-care institutions. Thus a quest for a "good death" emerged—a movement to improve how and where people die, and to reform a health-care system that considers death a failure and is focused on prolonging life.

Managing pain is one of the ways that the critically ill can die with dignity. In other words, the term *dignity* can guide doctors, patients, and their families in determining what kind of end-of-life care is appropriate for the dying person. End-of-life care may include addressing such issues as being a burden to others, settling one's affairs, getting spiritual comfort, maintaining privacy, easing anxiety, and obtaining physical relief from pain.

Numerous organizations today focus on dying-with-dignity issues. Some maintain websites and post articles on the subject, which can be found with the search term *dying with dignity*. One is Final Exit Network, a nonprofit organization with headquarters in Tallahassee, Florida. It operates throughout the United States. According to its website, the organization "provides education on all end of life choices as well as a compassionate presence to those who are suffering from incurable diseases and have chosen to end their suffering."[5] On their site, the Final Exit Network encourages people to have conversations with family, friends, and doctors about end-of-life choices.

Similar advice comes from Compassion and Choices, which says its "vision is a society where people receive state-of-the-art care and a full range of choices for dying in comfort, dignity and control. We aim to ensure individuals understand the risks and rewards of all feasible treatment options, treatment decisions are

National Healthcare Decisions Day

On April 16, 2016, the annual National Healthcare Decisions Day (NHDD) was observed. Sponsored by the National Hospice and Palliative Care Organization, NHDD is designed to educate the public and health-care providers about the importance of advance directives—documents that detail patients' wishes regarding end-of-life health care. A week-long theme for the 2017 NHDD event was "It Always Seems Too Early, Until It's Too Late." In other words, don't wait. Complete an advance directive document early in life. That advice applies to teenagers and young adults, not just middle-aged and older people. You can download your state's document from this website: http://www.caringinfo.org/i4a/pages/index.cfm?pageid=3289 or check the documents in the appendix of this book.

fully respected, and that care reflects a person's values and priorities for life's final chapter."[6]

Palliative Care

Palliative care is a philosophy—a way of thinking—about medical care for patients with life-threatening illness. It is comprehensive, specialized care provided by an interdisciplinary team, consisting of doctors, nurses, and other professional medical caregivers. The team provides ongoing comfort care for patients at home, or in an institution such as a hospital, extended care facility, or nursing home. Caregivers focus on alleviating a patient's pain and suffering. They also provide psychosocial and spiritual support.

Aly Becker was beginning her first year at the University of Iowa when she discovered how palliative care could benefit her. She had been diagnosed with "Eosinophilic Gastroenteropathy, a condition that causes white blood cells to build up in the gastro-intestinal system and the blood," according to an August 2016 report on GetPalliativeCare.org, which provides information for people coping with serious, complex illness. The website Aly's Story explained that towards the end of her last semester of freshman year, symptoms became too much to handle. The stomach issues continued to get worse despite her close attention to her diet, and eventually she had to take her meals through a feeding tube which she administered herself. Eventually, she was admitted to the hospital for closer attention.

"I think that's the turning point and sort of where I found myself just desperate for help in figuring out not just my physical symptoms, but also how to have the best quality of life and to make goals that were reachable and that weren't going to put my health and my life at risk," Aly said.[7]

She then turned to palliative care, and found "support for the depression and anxiety that stemmed from her illness. . . . She began seeing the team's chaplain to discuss spiritual matters and also worked with a musical therapist to express her emotions through song. These approaches had an immediate effect on Aly's well-being. She said, "It was the first time in a long time that I felt that there was any hope or any chance of making things better or finding a way to deal with my illness to the best of my ability.""[8]

Another young person who began receiving palliative care in 2016 was nineteen-year-old Stephon Wilson of Buffalo, New York. Stephon had a series of very serious health issues. After learning that he had an enlarged heart, he had a heart transplant in 2010. Over the next several years, he suffered "four heart attacks, a stroke and several seizures," and in 2016, his doctors "told him he would need a kidney transplant and another heart transplant, but he would not survive the surgeries," reported Christy Kern on News Chanel 4 WIVB. "Doctors told him to go home and make a bucket list"—a plan for things he'd always wanted to do, like go to a Broadway play and take a vacation. But he primarily planned to spend time with his family. "'All I can do is live life to the fullest [and] just try to make every day count,'" Stephon told the reporter.[9]

Hospice: A Movement and a Care System

Palliative and hospice care are similar in that they both provide combined care for patients through a single program—daily care, medications, equipment, and symptom treatment. "Where palliative care programs and hospice care programs differ greatly is in the care location, timing, payment, and eligibility for services," the CaregiversLibrary.org explains, adding, "Palliative care is for anyone with a serious illness. . . . It is not dependent on prognosis." Generally a person must be considered terminally ill or "within six months of death to be eligible for most hospice programs or to receive hospice benefits from insurance."[10]

The term *hospice* refers both to a movement and to a system of care. Hospices were first established in the Middle Ages in Europe, but at that time they were places where exhausted, ill, and dying travelers could find rest, food, and a roof over their heads. The hospices were found especially on routes to the Holy Land and were established to serve weary pilgrims and crusaders. In the sixteenth and seventeenth centuries, there were over one thousand hospices just in England and Scotland. In Dublin in 1879, a Catholic nun, Sister Mary Aitkenhead, opened what could be called the forerunner of modern hospice facilities, named Our Lady's Hospice. It was established primarily to care for terminally ill cancer patients and extended its services to help families of patients as well.

In 1960, a British physician named Dame Cicily Saunders proposed the revival of the hospice idea in caring for terminally ill patients. Her idea called for a peaceful place that would treat the spirit as well as provide palliative care. She opened St. Christopher's Hospice in London in 1967. The hospice philosophy, which has become increasingly popular in the United States, maintains that dying patients should have the ability to choose the way they would like to spend their remaining days.

The first hospice facility in America was established in New Haven, Connecticut, in 1974 by Dr. Sylvia Lack. Currently there are thousands of hospice facilities across the United States, in the Commonwealth of Puerto Rico and the Territory of Guam. Some hospices are stand-alone organizations; some are affiliated with hospitals. Many hospice patients are served in the privacy of their own homes, with medical personnel and volunteers making regular visits.

Hospice caregivers know that they are not the only factors in the patient's environment. Family members and friends are encouraged to provide additional support to the patient. But caregivers also realize that family and friends are undergoing considerable stress themselves due to their loved one's situation, and may also need various forms of help or counseling.

There are several national nonprofit organizations dedicated to promoting hospice ideals and information, such as the National Hospice and Palliative Care Organization, the Hospice Association of America, the National Association for Home Care and Hospice, and the Hospice Foundation of America.

Now You Know

Although the hospice movement developed out of Christian traditions, the philosophy respects all religious orientations, atheism, and agnosticism. It does not seek to convert or change participants to any particular religious belief.

Hospice Volunteers

Because Hospice organizations must be able to provide all essential services twenty-four hours a day, seven days a week, they need volunteers who may include professional health-care workers donating skilled medical care, or community members performing such duties as reading to patients or cooking for patients and their families. Volunteers may also provide managerial help, such as computer data entry, fiscal management, or communication assistance.

Hospice teams encourage high school and college students to take part in volunteer programs. Wherever students serve as hospice volunteers, their hours and duties are usually flexible. Some volunteers may run errands for patients and their families. They might encourage patients to record their life stories on videos. Or they could help with patient birthday parties, play music, share baked goods, or help out with office tasks.

Kara Smith of Scottsdale signed up to be one of Arizona's Hospice of the Valley (HOV) volunteers. She noted, "When my initial visit was over with my patient, he made me promise I would come back. Sharing stories, reading and just being together with someone who deeply appreciates the time we spend with them makes being an HOV volunteer a unique experience. Even though I spend one hour a week with my patient, to him it is timeless."[11]

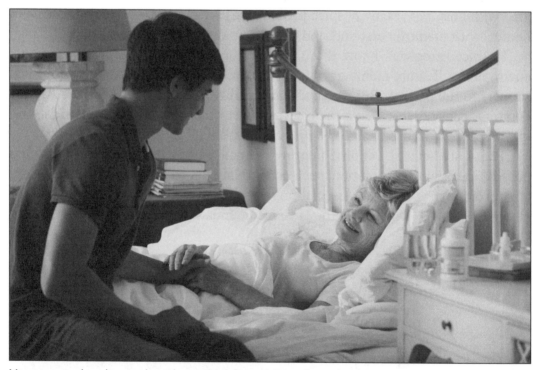

Young people who are hospice volunteers visit patients in their homes, hospitals, nursing homes, or other medical facilities. © iStock.com/bowdenimages

Another HOV volunteer, Nhi Van of Phoenix, declared, "Hospice is a place where I feel like it's my second family. Knowing that I can help other people, especially at the end of their lives, is really amazing. It makes you smile from the inside out."[12]

Rachel in Montgomery County, Maryland, became a volunteer at Montgomery Hospice, and explained, "When I decided to join Montgomery Hospice as a volunteer, most of my college friends expressed disbelief: 'Why would you want to do that? That sounds so depressing!' At nineteen, I think it is safe to say that I am one of the youngest volunteers at Montgomery Hospice. I decided to volunteer for hospice for two main reasons: My best friend's mom received care through Montgomery Hospice a couple of years ago. I had never heard of end-of-life care, and I was impressed by the compassionate support that the hospice team provided."[13]

After serving as hospice volunteers, many young people decide to make nursing a career. Brooke Liston, for example, was a teen volunteer at Suncoast Hospice in Pinellas County, Florida. "Her service included patient and family support, office, community outreach, special events, craft meetings, teen council, holiday caroling and baking," according to Ebony Faber, writing for Suncoast's network of care known as Empath Health. In an interview Brooke said, "Going into nursing was definitely due in huge part to Suncoast Hospice. I loved working and talking with the patients. It directed me toward nursing."[14]

Brooke attended the University of Florida and graduated with honors in 2016. She began work in the nurse residency program at Cleveland Clinic in Ohio. "At Cleveland Clinic, we have that bedside care with all the highs and lows of the patients, and I love it," Brooke said in the interview. "Sometimes we get patients who go into palliative care when they are very sick and treatments are no longer effective. I always use my hospice experience. I learned so much from hospice, whether it's communicating with patients or compassion. I still think about it every time I work."[15]

Bioethics

Hospice and palliative care are guided by a discipline known as bioethics, which deals with ethical matters in medical treatments and practices. The field of bioethics, or medical ethics, has been continually evolving since the days of ancient Greek philosophers, although the term *bioethics* was not coined until the 1970s. Bioethics today deals with the moral implications of medical decisions, research, and treatments, which have become increasingly complex given the developments in science and medical technology over the past few decades.

For hospice and palliative care nurses, bioethics is an "ethic of care and caring. In no area is this more evident than in the care of those with progressive debilitating disease and those at the end of life," wrote Nessa Coyle in the *Journal of Hospice and Palliative Nursing*. She explained that nurses encounter ethical issues "daily while providing palliative and hospice care." Coyle noted that some of the ethical issues hospice nurses encounter include determining whether life support for the terminally ill is "in the best interests of the patient" and "inadequate communication about end-of-life care between providers, patients, and families." Nurses also have to deal with ethical questions about how much pain relief to provide for patients and how to proceed when patients have not completed advance directives or the hospital ignores a patient's instructions about end-of-life care.[16]

Bioethics is also a field of study at biomedical centers and universities across the United States and in other countries. One of the most well-known centers is the independent nonprofit Hastings Institute in Garrison, New York. Alan Meisel, JD, noted on the institute's website that "end-of-life care and its many dilemmas capture public attention when they make national news. The story often involves a family seeking a court order to remove life support from a patient who, medical experts say, is in a vegetative state with no hope of recovery. . . . When the news fades, so does public attention to end-of-life decisions. In reality, however, these decisions are omnipresent." For those "who live out their final days in hospitals, nursing homes, and at home in hospice care, decisions must continually be made about what treatment to administer, what treatment to cease or withhold, what treatment to continue, and what treatment to taper off." Thus "end-of-life decision-making occupies center stage in contemporary American bioethics."[17]

Other bioethical concerns have focused on patient informed consent, euthanasia, managed medical care, organ transplants, public health priorities, questionable surgeries, mistreatment of human subjects in medical research, treatment of animals in research, and many more issues. Bioethics also is involved in lawmaking because the consequences of medical research and health care could infringe on civil and privacy rights. The important point in bioethics is that legal requirements should not replace ethical values in medical care.

EUTHANASIA: MERCY KILLING OR MURDER?

"People deserve the right to determine their own destiny.
Euthanasia should be made a legal alternative for terminally-ill patients."
—*Erica in an essay for* Teen Ink[1]

In the United States and other industrialized countries, euthanasia sometimes is called "mercy killing" because it hastens death for suffering, terminally ill patients. The term *euthanasia* comes from the Greek phrase eu thanatos, meaning "well death," or dying without pain. In many instances, euthanasia involves a physician who provides the means for a person to end his or her life.

In June 2015, the *Economist* and Ipsos MORI, a market research organization, polled attitudes toward doctor-assisted dying in fifteen countries. In the poll, majorities in thirteen countries

thought doctor-assisted dying should be legal for adults. Western Europe was broadly more supportive than eastern Europe. Large majorities were in favour in Belgium and the Netherlands, where doctor-assisted dying is legal, and—much more surprisingly—in France and Spain, where it is not, and the Catholic church's influence is strong. When people were asked to think about the specifics of how a life should be taken, support fell considerably, though in nine countries it remained above 50%. . . . And for terminally ill children, few were willing to allow it. Belgium, the only country with no lower age limit, stood alone in having a majority, or near-majority, in favour for all three age groups we asked about: under-tens, 11- to 14-year-olds and 15- to 17-year-olds.[2]

Although not part of a poll, numerous teenagers have expressed their pro and con opinions regarding euthanasia. Four examples follow, two supporting euthanasia and two against it.

Sean of Massachusetts put it this way in *Teen Ink*:

> Euthanasia . . . is a good idea. . . . If I ever get old and really sick I hope euthanasia will be legal, because if I'm suffering, I don't want to drag it out. If you think about it, euthanasia could actually save lives. If an eighteen-year-old kid gets into a car accident and has no chance to live outside the hospital, why not use his organs for people who need them. If the kid's parents don't have the money or don't want the kid to live a life of pain, let the kid help someone else.[3]

In another *Teen Ink* essay, Erika P. states, "Euthanasia is a method of expressing control over one's own body and should be legalized. It is a process that allows a terminally-ill patient to terminate his or her life on request. For decades, euthanasia has been considered inhumane and immoral. How can one say they are a humanitarian if they force a grief-stricken, terminally-ill patient to suffer a prolonged illness when they would prefer the settlement of death?"[4]

A teen against euthanasia, Sarah Klammer, published her view in *Clearly Caring* magazine and posted it online in 2011 when she was sixteen years old. At the time, Sarah, her mother, and sisters were volunteers at a nursing home in their hometown Frankenmuth, Michigan. Sarah noted that she often heard patients' relatives and the facility's staff

> talk about what a blessing it is when [a resident] "finally" passes away, as if the resident had no purpose while at the nursing home. I also hear the news about euthanasia and how maybe, when "quality of life" is gone, the person should be too—but I don't believe it. I don't believe it because I see "purpose" every time I'm at the home, if nothing else, in how much my sisters and I learn from every resident we see. I don't know how people can think they know what God's will is in this world, what purpose He has for each of us, or how long our lives should last on this earth. Just as every resident at the home is different, so must be the plan for each of us.[5]

Kara, who was a student at Hawaii Community College in 2011, posted on Generations for Life her objections to euthanasia and doctor-assisted suicide. She wrote, "If euthanasia were to be legalized, the Equal Protection Clause of the 14th Amendment would require that incompetent people be given the same right, which could lead to abuses and involuntary euthanasia. . . . I challenge you to reevaluate your ideas about euthanasia and physician-assisted suicide. I hope

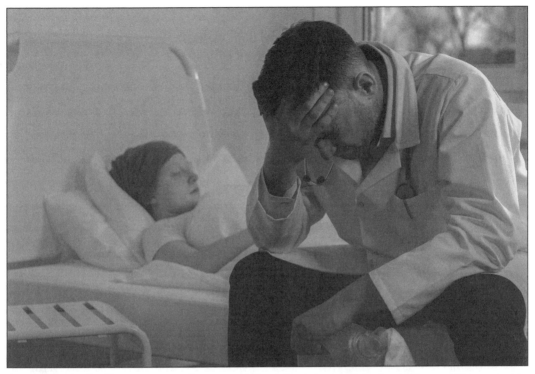

Some terminally ill young people may ask for physician-assisted suicide, creating a quandary for doctors who oppose euthanasia even when it is legal in their state. © *iStock.com/KatarzynaBialasiewicz*

It Happened to Valentina

A Chilean teenager, fourteen-year-old Valentina Maureira, made worldwide news in February 2015 when she produced a YouTube video, pleading for permission to die. She suffered from cystic fibrosis, a disease that killed her brother at the age of six. Cystic fibrosis causes damage to vital organs, and people with the disease seldom survive beyond age twenty or thirty.

On the video, which has been seen by millions, Valentina directed her message to the Chilean president, Michelle Bachelet (a pediatrician): "I urgently request to speak to the president because I'm tired of living with this illness. . . . I want her approval so I can get a shot that will make me sleep forever," she said.[a]

Bachelet turned down the request, explaining that euthanasia is illegal in Chile. However, the president visited Valentina in the hospital and told her that the state would provide psychiatric care and help with medicines, if Valentina needed them. The teenager and the president were photographed and pictures of them were posted on the Internet.

The publicity prompted an Argentinian woman to visit Valentina. She had cystic fibrosis and was in her twenties, giving Valentina hope that she might also live longer. Soon after the visit, Valentina announced that she had changed her mind and no longer wanted to be euthanized. Sadly, however, she suffered complications of the disease and on May 15, 2015, she died.

that you will decide, as I did, that the cost of legalizing [euthanasia] isn't worth the cost we could ultimately pay" for allowing someone else to help you die.[6]

Changes in Beliefs about Euthanasia

The ancient Greeks had fairly well-defined beliefs about eu thantos and bringing about their own or someone else's death. Killing oneself or helping another die could only be done for acceptable reasons. A person who wished to die had to be seriously ill with a painful disease, overcome with grief, in disgrace, or condemned to die. Suicide and euthanasia were considered ignoble if committed for cowardly reasons as determined by the culture.

In 399 BC, the ancient Greek philosopher Socrates was charged with vague crimes such as irreverence, worshipping new gods, and corrupting the youth of Athens with his teachings. These crimes were punishable by death. Influential friends offered to help him escape and flee Athens, but Socrates refused, believing he should honor the law. So he voluntarily drank a liquid with lethal hemlock, which at the time was a common form of administering the death penalty.

From about the fourteenth century on, people's ideas about euthanasia began to change. As new medical and scientific knowledge made it possible to extend life, philosophers and physicians wrote about and discussed humane or less painful ways of dying. Some argued against medical intervention that lengthened the dying process and called for the use of drugs such as morphine to ease suffering and even to bring about a merciful death. A few even proposed that active euthanasia should be a legal option available for patients with painful and incurable ailments.

During the late 1800s and early 1900s, it was not unusual for medical and legal scholars in Europe and the United States to actively promote the idea of mercy killing and people's right to decide for themselves when they would die. Doctors

The Greek philosopher Socrates, who is commemorated with this statue, killed himself by ingesting a poisonous concoction. © iStock.com/sedmak

became increasingly concerned about their responsibility to act on behalf of dying patients who were tortured by pain.

Views changed once again during World War II (1939–1945) when Americans and Europeans learned about the horrific, despicable acts of the Nazis under German dictator Adolf Hitler. The Nazis launched a secret euthanasia program that they claimed was mercy killing but was actually a calculated and cruel extermination of people the Nazis labeled "useless eaters." Millions of Jews, Romas,

The Hippocratic Oath

In euthanasia debates, opponents often refer to the Hippocratic Oath, purportedly written by the ancient Greek physician Hippocrates, considered the father of medicine. Scholars have long disputed the original Greek wording of the oath, and translations have varied. In addition, some interpretations reflect the many changes in medicine and culture over the 2,500 years since the oath was written.

Basically, the oath is a promise to the gods to care for the sick, preserve the privacy of a patient, and teach medical practices to the next generation. Some euthanasia opponents emphasize that the oath obligates physicians not to give deadly medicine to anyone if asked and not to advise anyone in that regard—in other words, to preserve life and not hasten death.

Although it is commonly believed that medical students swear to the Hippocratic Oath during graduation ceremonies, instead they are likely to recite or read in their programs a modern version of the oath—a pledge that reflects today's medical realities. In fact, a revised oath that is most often used was written in 1964 by Louis Lasagna, academic dean of the School of Medicine at Tufts University. Using this version, a medical school graduate pledges in part to apply the measures needed to benefit the sick, avoiding overtreatment; to remember that sympathy and understanding are an important part of medicine; to call in colleagues when their skills are needed; to respect patient privacy and to be especially careful when treating life-and-death matters; and finally to treat a patient not as a chart or medical record but as a sick person "whose illness may affect the person's family and economic stability."[b]

Hippocrates 460-377 B.C.
father of medicine

15c TRANSKEI

C1.4 1982

This postage stamp from Transkei, South Africa, honors Hippocrates, called the father of medicine and said to be the author of the Hippocratic Oath. © *iStock.com/PictureLake*

homosexuals, mentally and physically disabled, and others whom Hitler considered valueless were murdered. Today, opponents of euthanasia fear that if mercy killing is allowed, eventually governments may set up programs to do away with unwanted members of society just as Hitler did.

Kevorkian: Early Advocate for Assisted Suicide

Dr. Jack Kevorkian (1928–2011) was a longtime supporter of assisted suicide, and his actions prompted early debates about the morality and legality of physician-assisted suicide. A retired Michigan pathologist and trained physician, Kevorkian believed that people have a right to avoid a lingering, miserable death by ending their own lives with help from a doctor who can ensure that they die peacefully.

Throughout the 1980s Kevorkian published numerous articles on euthanasia. He also advertised in newspapers as a medical death counselor for anyone who wished to die with dignity. In 1989 he used scrap parts to build what he called the thanatron, a Greek term for death machine and better known in news articles as a suicide machine. It consisted of three glass bottles inside a frame connected to an intravenous tube. The device allowed a person to ingest first a harmless saline solution, then a sedative, and finally a lethal drug.

Janet Adkins of Portland, Oregon, was the first person to contact Kevorkian about ending her life. Adkins was a victim of Alzheimer's disease and she wanted to plan her death while she was still mentally competent. At first Kevorkian refused to assist in her suicide, but in 1990 Adkins and her husband, Ron, convinced him to help Janet end her life with his suicide machine.

Once Adkins's death was reported, public reaction—both pro and con—was explosive. Kevorkian was arrested and charged with murder, but the judge dismissed the case on the grounds that Michigan had no law against doctor-assisted suicide. The controversy became more intense when Kevorkian helped two other women die in 1991. The state board of medicine revoked Kevorkian's medical license, and police charged Kevorkian with the murder of the women. But once again charges were dropped because no law prohibited Kevorkian's actions.

Meanwhile, Kevorkian helped many other people commit suicide. Finally, the Michigan legislature passed a law, which went into effect in 1993, banning assisted suicide. Nevertheless, Kevorkian continued to assist people who wanted to die.

In 1999, Thomas Youk requested Kevorkian's help to administer a lethal injection of drugs. Youk was fifty-four years old and in the advanced stages of amyotrophic lateral sclerosis, or Lou Gehrig's disease, which eventually causes paralysis. Kevorkian made a videotape showing him injecting Youk with a lethal drug and sent it to CBS's *60 Minutes*.

After the tape was broadcast, Michigan authorities charged Kevorkian with first-degree murder and delivering a controlled substance without a license. Kevorkian was convicted and sentenced to ten to twenty-five years in prison. Kevorkian's lawyer repeatedly appealed his client's conviction in Michigan courts but was denied. So the next appeal went to the U.S. Supreme Court in 2002, but the High Court refused to hear it. In 2007, Kevorkian was released on parole, promising that he would not assist in a suicide of another person. He died in 2011 at the age of eighty-three.

Passive and Active Euthanasia

In the debate over euthanasia, medical personnel, theologians, bioethicists, and many nonprofessionals make a distinction between passive and active euthanasia. In general, passive euthanasia is allowing a person to die by withholding or withdrawing medical treatment. Respirators, heart and lung machines, feeding tubes, and other mechanical means of maintaining life are withdrawn or not used when there is no known chance that a patient will be cured. The idea is to stop treatment and shorten the dying process, preventing a prolonged death.

Active euthanasia is a much more complex and controversial matter. It usually involves a terminally ill person in extreme, unrelieved pain, who uses lethal medical treatment (injections or pills) or who asks someone else to take the action to end suffering or hasten death (assisted suicide). When a doctor helps a patient commit suicide, it is called physician-assisted suicide (PAS). In recent years in the United States, there has been a growing debate about whether mature adults have the right to terminate their lives when their suffering becomes unbearable. In countries such as the Netherlands, Belgium, and Luxemburg when a patient is terminally ill and suffering greatly, it is permissible for a physician to assist that person in ending his or her life. Physicians may legally offer medically acceptable drugs, including the one used to terminate the lives of unwanted cats and dogs.

Many of those who seek help in ending their lives are people with incurable and agonizing diseases such as AIDS, severe respiratory ailments, and cancer. The largest group of Americans who ask for assistance in dying are the elderly, according to federal studies. A number of cases of husbands or wives helping their ailing spouses die (mercy killings) have been reported in the media. In some instances the surviving spouse also commits suicide in order to avoid prosecution.

In almost every U.S. state, assisted suicide is a crime. Oregon was the first to pass a landmark law allowing assisted suicide. Called the Death with Dignity Act of 1994, it was not immediately implemented because opponents sought and received a legal injunction against it. The Ninth Circuit Court of Appeals lifted the injunction on October 27, 1997, and PAS then became a legal option for terminally ill patients in the state. In 2001, U.S. attorney general John Ashcroft blocked Oregon's assisted suicide law and authorized federal drug agents to arrest doctors who prescribe lethal drugs for dying patients. Two days later, the action was suspended by a temporary restraining order. In 2002, U.S. district judge Robert Jones ruled that the U.S. Justice Department lacked the authority to overturn the Oregon law, allowing it to remain intact. That action encouraged other states to pass similar laws.

Washington State passed a law like Oregon's in 2008. In Montana, a court ruling in 2009 shields physicians if they assist patients who request help in dying. Vermont legalized assisted suicide in 2013 as did California in 2015 and Colorado in 2016. In October 2016, the District of Columbia also legalized euthanasia. Other states have proposed bills legalizing assisted suicide but as of March 2017, no other states have passed euthanasia laws.

Opponents of Assisted Suicide

Opponents of assisted suicide and euthanasia argue that any person who aids or permits the killing of other humans is committing murder. They frequently point out that those who ask for assistance in dying may change their minds or find medical help that improves their lives.

Advocates for the disabled have long argued that assisted suicide could lead to killing people with severe physical disabilities, the mentally ill, developmentally disabled, and fragile elderly. Disability activists founded Not Dead Yet (NDY) in 1996. The organization opposes legalizing assisted suicide and euthanasia in the United States. Shortly after it organized, NDY rallied in Washington, DC, where a reported five hundred people with disabilities chanted "Not Dead Yet" in opposition to two assisted suicide cases being heard by the U.S. Supreme Court. NDY along with other national disability organizations denounces assisted suicide as the ultimate form of discrimination. In the view of NDY, any proposed law authorizing PAS targets individuals based on their health status in violation of the Americans with Disabilities Act. Although many civil rights and health care advocates argue that individual autonomy is at the core of movements to legalize assisted suicide, disabled people say that U.S. health-care and legal systems do not guarantee them equal protection of the law.

Bouvia v. Superior Court

The court case *Bouvia v. Superior Court* (1986) is often cited in college courses on ethical issues in health care. Elizabeth Bouvia was born with severe cerebral palsy and at the age of ten her mother placed her in Angel View Crippled Children's Foundation home in Desert Hot Springs, California. When she was eighteen, she was able to leave and use a motorized wheelchair and eventually graduated from college and married.

When she was in her twenties, she had very limited muscle control and was in constant pain from arthritis and contractures. She had suffered a miscarriage, the breakup of her marriage, and the drowning death of her brother. She also learned that her mother had cancer.

In 1985, she wanted to die. She checked herself into a hospital in Riverside, California, requesting relief from pain and care while she starved herself. Doctors instead ordered that she be force-fed or discharged from the hospital. Richard Scott, a lawyer and pro-euthanasia group, presented Bouvia's case to the California Superior Court. The court found her competent and her decision rational, but ruled that she did not have the right to assisted suicide.

The case then went to the Court of Appeals, which overruled the Superior Court decision and also cited the High Court ruling that "for purposes of this case, it is assumed that a competent person would have a constitutionally protected right to refuse lifesaving hydration and nutrition." Bouvia's case took at least two years to go through the court system, and during that time a doctor advised Bouvia that aggressive pain management was available. She accepted the doctor's care and changed her mind about ending her life.[c]

Other disability organizations that oppose legalized suicide include the American Disabled for Attendant Programs Today, American Association of People with Disabilities, Autistic Self Advocacy Network, Disability Rights Center, National Council on Disability, National Spinal Cord Injury Association, United Spinal Association, and others.

Persistent Vegetative State

A related euthanasia issue is the controversy over removing life support for someone who is medically determined to be in a persistent vegetative state (PVS) or brain dead. A person who is diagnosed as brain dead has no neurological activity in the brain and brain stem, but the body's vital organs are maintained with a ventilator and feeding and hydration tubes.

When a PVS patient loses functions of the brain and brainstem, spontaneous movements may occur. The patient's eyes may open in response to external stimuli. She or he may occasionally grimace, cry, or laugh, but cannot speak or obey commands. In brief, the patient may appear somewhat normal, but has no mental abilities and has only reflex actions.

The PVS condition sometimes follows a coma, or deep state of unconsciousness, due to a complication of an illness, lack of oxygen to the brain when a person suffers a stroke or heart attack, or head injury.

Most medical experts insist that if the brain dies, a live person no longer exists and it is futile and expensive to continue mechanical support. They also argue that the financial burden of a PVS patient can devastate families, and that it is morally justifiable to discontinue life-prolonging measures; resources and funds could be better used for patients who have a realistic chance for improvement. Others argue that it is immoral to cut off life support such as a ventilator, hydration, and feeding tube; they insist that a PVS patient is still alive.

Another issue focuses on whether the vegetative state is actually permanent; cases have occurred in which patients have recovered more than a year after being diagnosed as in a persistent vegetative state. Members of many religious communities believe that PVS patients should be maintained with life support systems because even though their condition is tragic, they are still persons and like all humans need nourishment and fluids to remain alive. The opposing position is that PVS patients function only at a reflexive level. Because their brains are not functioning, there is little hope of recovery, so their lives should not be prolonged. Several legal cases in the past decades focused attention on young people who were medically determined to be in a persistent vegetative state: Karen Ann Quinlan, Nancy Cruzan, and Terri Schiavo.

Karen Ann Quinlan

The case of Karen Ann Quinlan (1954–1985) of New Jersey prompted additional U.S. debates over the right to die. In 1975, twenty-one-year-old Karen Ann went to a birthday party. For several days prior to the party, she had eaten little and also had taken some drugs—perhaps tranquilizers, but that is not certain. At the party, Karen Ann consumed a few alcoholic drinks and suddenly began to act strangely. Her friends took her to their home. Later, when they checked on her, they found she was not breathing and called a rescue squad who rushed her to a hospital.

Karen Ann's breathing was restored and she was connected to a respirator. But the lack of oxygen during the time when her breathing was interrupted caused permanent brain damage. She was in a coma, but was not considered brain dead. Karen Ann's electroencephalogram showed that she had brain-wave activity and also responded to stimuli. A neurologist ordered continued use of the respirator and nourishment through a feeding tube.

Karen Ann's parents were convinced their daughter would not want to be kept alive by artificial means. After conferring with their priest, they asked the doctor to disconnect their daughter's respirator. But the doctor refused on the grounds that he would be committing murder. Believing they should be able to act on their daughter's behalf, the Quinlans sued the hospital. A superior court judge ruled that the state, through the hospital, had a duty to continue life support for Karen Ann; her parents could not determine her fate. But in a 1976 appeal to the New Jersey Supreme Court, the lower court ruling was overturned. The higher court said that Karen Ann's right to privacy—the right to make her own decisions—had been infringed and that her parents could assert this right for her. As a result, she was removed from the respirator and taken to a nursing home.

Many medical personnel thought Karen Ann would die without a machine to help her breathe, but instead her body continued to live. She was kept alive with nourishment delivered through the feeding tube. Her parents believed that food and water should be provided, even though some experts argued then and argue still that forced feedings are just another artificial means of maintaining a life that is more like that of a vegetable than of a person. In other words, Karen Ann was in a persistent vegetative state, or permanent coma. She remained in this condition for ten years. In 1985, her body died.

Nancy Cruzan

Nancy Cruzan became the subject of a well-publicized right-to-die case in Missouri. Nancy was twenty-five years old when she had a car accident in 1983. She was driving on an icy road when her car slid off the road, hit trees and a mailbox, and overturned. Nancy was thrown from the vehicle and landed unconscious face down in a ditch. Her breathing stopped for an estimated twelve to fourteen minutes before paramedics arrived and restored her breathing and heartbeat. But she had been without oxygen for six minutes, which meant her brain was not functioning, doctors determined. Nancy remained in a coma for approximately three weeks and then progressed to an unconscious state. She was able to orally ingest some nutrition. But to ease feeding and further the recovery, surgeons implanted a feeding and hydration tube in Nancy.

After ten months Nancy had not gained consciousness and was transferred to a long-term care facility. She exhibited motor reflexes, her eyes opened and closed, but she showed no signs of significant brain functions. One year after Nancy's accident, her husband felt he needed to go on with his life and filed for divorce. Nancy's parents, Joe and Joyce Cruzan, became her legal guardians.

After Joe and Joyce Cruzan learned that their daughter would never regain her mental faculties, they requested that all Nancy's life supports be removed. They were convinced that their daughter would not want to be kept alive with machines. But medical personnel refused to withdraw food and water without a court order, arguing that if these were not provided as basic care, they would be killing Nancy by starvation and dehydration.

In 1988, the Cruzans, acting on Nancy's behalf, obtained a circuit court ruling that the feeding tube could be removed. But the Missouri attorney general appealed the case to the Missouri Supreme Court, which overturned the lower court ruling. The higher court concluded that the state could abide by only the patient's declared wishes, not by surrogates'. Under Missouri law, the court said, Joe and Joyce Cruzan did not have the authority to act for their daughter. Since the state had the responsibility to protect life, food and water were required as basic care.

Over the next few years, the Cruzans visited their daughter regularly, but were constantly frustrated that she could not achieve a peaceful ending. They, along with their two other daughters and many of Nancy's friends, believed that Nancy had died in the car accident and the feeding and dehydration tubes were only keeping her body alive.

The Cruzan case eventually reached the U.S. Supreme Court (*Cruzan v. Director, Missouri Department of Health*). In 1990, the justices ruled that a person has the constitutional right to refuse life-support treatment, including food and water. It was a historic decision, the first high court ruling on this issue, which, in effect, said a person has a right to die without interference. But the justices also declared that any state could limit that right for incompetent persons. The case was remanded back to Missouri.

The Cruzans were granted a second hearing before the county court judge who had originally ruled on their case. Several of Nancy's former coworkers testified for the first time about long conversations they had had with Nancy, who clearly stated that she would not want to be kept alive by artificial means. Two coworkers said they had not come forward years before because they had not known about the case.

Because of the testimony, the county judge ruled that Nancy Cruzan's wishes were clear and convincing, as required by the Supreme Court. On December 14, 1990, her feeding tube was removed. Protest groups had tried last-minute legal maneuvers to prevent the removal of the feeding tube. When those failed, they invaded the hospital to try to reconnect the apparatus and even threatened to take Nancy away. But the comatose woman was allowed to exist without life support. Her family maintained their vigil until Nancy died on December 26, 1990.

Terri Schiavo

Another PVS case that received widespread national attention was that of Terri Schiavo of Tampa, Florida. In 1990 Terri had a heart attack and oxygen to her brain was cut off, leaving her in a persistent vegetative state. She was provided nutrition and hydration through a feeding tube. Although she had cyclical periods of wakefulness and sleep, eye and facial movements, and emitted cries and moans, her doctors said these actions were involuntary reflexes, not signs of emotional or intellectual activity.

Terri's husband, Michael Schiavo, argued that his wife would not want to live in this condition and requested that her feeding tube be removed and her body allowed to die. But Terri's parents, Bob and Mary Schindler, argued that their daughter should be kept alive, that she responded to their daily visits, and that there were possibilities she could be revived. Court cases followed over many years, with doctors testifying for both sides. Then Florida governor Jeb Bush inserted himself into the controversy and applied political pressure on a circuit court judge to require that Terri's life support be maintained. The judge ruled in November 2002 that no current medical practice could change Terri Schiavo's condition and ordered that her feeding tube be removed on January 3, 2003. After more than twelve years, her body was allowed to rest in peace.

The Continued Debate

Ever since the decisions regarding Karen Ann Quinlan, Nancy Cruzan, and Terri Schiavo, the controversies over PVS and the right to die have continued. Although there has been an increase in the number of Americans who say they approve of legalizing euthanasia, there has not been a significant spike in reported PAS. In fact, a study by researchers at the Perelman School of Medicine at the University of Pennsylvania noted in 2016 that euthanasia and PAS worldwide are "relatively rare." A news release noted,

> Analysis revealed that in U.S. jurisdictions where the practices are legal, less than 20 percent of physicians report receiving requests for euthanasia or PAS, and less than five percent have complied. In Oregon and Washington state, less than one percent of licensed physicians write prescriptions for PAS, and in the vast majority of cases, patients are already or had previously received hospice care. Belgium and the Netherlands also report a positive association between euthanasia and receiving or consulting with palliative care teams or pain specialists.[7]

The news release noted that the leading researcher for the study was Ezekiel J. Emanuel, MD, who said that data from the study "strongly suggests that the dominant motivations for requesting euthanasia or PAS are loss of autonomy and dignity, the inability to enjoy life and regular activities, or other mental illnesses, rather than physical pain. . . . However, given the incomplete and outdated information available about the practices of assisted dying, collecting reliable data to evaluate end-of-life practices should be prioritized around the world, not just in countries legalizing euthanasia or PAS."[8] Yet, no matter how much data is collected, the national debate over euthanasia is likely to continue for decades to come.

SUICIDE LOSS AND SURVIVAL

....

"After my [suicide] attempt I needed to be able to talk and be heard—
not counseled, not encouraged—to really be listened to, like what I had
to say was the most important thing in the world at that moment, for
someone to connect to my pain without losing control of themselves."
—Cathy Singer in A Journey Toward Health and Hope[1]

The U.S. suicide rates were on the rise in 2016—so said numerous news accounts across the nation. People of all ages, economic, social, and ethnic backgrounds intentionally kill themselves. A report from the Centers for Disease Control and Prevention (CDC) noted that in 2016 there were a total of 42,773 U.S. deaths from suicide, including 21,334 from firearms, 11,407 from suffocation, and 6,808 from poisoning.[2] Other means were not categorized.

It is one thing to look at data, but quite another to learn about people who were once happily alive but took their own lives. Connor Ball was one adolescent who suddenly and apparently without warning died by his own hand. He was an active fourteen-year-old, living in Brentwood, New Hampshire, in 2011. Both of his parents, John and Tara Ball, had airline jobs and Connor was able to travel with them at times, visiting many places around the globe. A student at Exeter High School, Connor was an honor student, hockey player, and on his way to becoming an Eagle Scout. He was also an avid Red Sox fan. He appeared to be living a happy, gregarious life with little down time.

However, in the fall of 2011, he became one of the suicide statistics. He died by hanging, according to the state medical examiner's office. Only after the terrible shock did his family learn about Connor's depression. In 2016, John Ball told NBC reporter Emma Margolin that he had had five years to think about his son's depression and death. "I have racked my brain trying to understand the reason." To deal with their heartbreak, John and Tara Ball, along with family and friends, established a nonprofit called Connor's Climb Foundation to raise awareness of suicide by establishing a Signs of Suicide (SOS) program, which is free of charge to New Hampshire schools. SOS is a depression awareness and suicide prevention program for middle schools and high schools.[3]

Live-Streaming Suicides

A suicide of a Miami-Dade high school student, who was in foster care, was shown on an appalling Facebook live video in late January 2017. Many people—the exact number is unknown—watched this live-streaming, two-hour video, in which fourteen-year-old Naika Venant hanged herself. The suicide happened late Sunday night, January 22, while her foster parents were sleeping. She created a noose out of a scarf and attached it to the frame of her bathroom shower door. While the video played, some Facebook viewers ridiculed Naika, called her insulting names, and posted videos showing mock hangings of themselves. That video was soon deleted from Facebook. Some viewers blamed the website for allowing the video on the site.

Reporting the story in the *Tampa Bay Times*, Leonard Pitts wrote,

> The harsh laughter and cold ridicule of "people"—the word is used advisedly—who watched Naika's suicide suggest that we flatter ourselves when we call ourselves a higher species. Apparently, only one individual tried to help; a friend saw the live feed and called police, but inadvertently sent them to the wrong address. By the time it got sorted out, Naika was beyond saving. . . . Facebook is an easy target [to blame], but it is not the web service whose behavior is appalling here. It is, rather, the ordinary people, the everyday Janes and Joes who could have acted to save this child, but did not. One is mindful of what's called "the bystander effect," which, according to *Psychology Today*, "occurs when the presence of others hinders an individual from intervening in an emergency situation."[4]

Just weeks before Naika's death, another young girl had live-streamed her suicide. According to a report in the *Miami Herald*, "12-year-old Katelyn Nicole Davis of Cedartown, Ga., killed herself in a 40-minute live video. The video was posted through a site called live.me and was taken down by family members as soon as relatives became aware. . . . While the video was live, viewers saved versions of it and posted them elsewhere, including on Facebook."[5]

There appear to be no conclusive reasons for live-streaming a suicide, but apparently some young people want attention and fame after their death. Others may be seeking revenge—now-see-what-you-made-me-do kind of payback to a family member, former friend, teacher, or classmate. Or they may be influenced

A sign in front of the Golden Gate Bridge in San Francisco urges anyone contemplating suicide to get crisis counseling. © *iStock.com/frontpoint*

by what they perceive as the way to end their misery in a copycat action. As with all suicides the reasons are complex and intertwined.

Suicide Attempts

Beyond the total number of suicides annually, no statistics are kept on suicide attempts in the United States. Survivors usually try to hide their history of attempted suicide "because of the abuse and bullying they will receive," as a female on SuicideFindingHope.com reported. "Survivors like me get called psycho, crazy, insane . . . Etc. guys won't date me. I have been sober from suicide for 4 years now, but I can't celebrate it because [I'll] be shunned."[6]

One person among those inflicting self-harm in attempted suicide was a Florida student at Gainesville High School. In 2015, Rachel Abrams participated in a teen poetry event and read her contribution that focused on a time "when she was hospitalized with severe depression and considered suicide." According to a news report, Rachel said, "I'm sitting on the bathroom floor with a razor blade in one hand and the doctor's number in the other. Which do I choose?" Months later, she says, "I finally love myself the way I'm supposed to. . . . Now I have so much to live for—myself."[7]

> ### Suicide Data
>
> The American Foundation for Suicide Prevention, using CDC data, noted that in 2014,
>
> 494,169 people visited a hospital for injuries due to self-harm. This number suggests that approximately 12 people harm themselves for every reported death by suicide. However, because of the way these data are collected, we are not able to distinguish intentional suicide attempts from non-intentional self-harm behaviors. Many suicide attempts, however, go unreported or untreated. Surveys suggest that at least one million people in the U.S. each year engage in intentionally inflicted self-harm.
>
> Females attempt suicide three times more often than males. As with suicide deaths, rates of attempted suicide vary considerably among demographic groups. While males are 4 times more likely than females to die by suicide, females attempt suicide 3 times as often as males. The ratio of suicide attempts to suicide death in youth is estimated to be about 25:1, compared to about 4:1 in the elderly.[a]

A booklet titled *A Journey Toward Help and Hope: Your Handbook for Recovery after a Suicide Attempt*, explains that diverse causes or events can lead to a suicide attempt, but "a common theme that many suicide attempt survivors report is the need to feel relief. At desperate moments, when it feels like nothing else is working, suicide may seem like the only way to get relief from unbearable emotional pain." The booklet, available free of charge from the U.S. Department of Health and Human Services, includes a story about teenager Jordan Burham, who at age sixteen had been diagnosed with depression. According to the story, Jordan, an African American, "was popular and had almost everything he wanted" but "said that he hated himself."

He felt that he didn't fit in with the mostly white students in his school, and he felt like a failure if he didn't get the grades he and his parents wanted him to achieve. He went to therapy for his depression . . . but he didn't talk honestly with his therapist. He didn't take his medications consistently and kept his drinking problem a secret. After his suicide attempt, he ended up in a hospital . . . in a coma, and his doctors didn't know if he would survive. When Jordan woke up, he had to heal physically and went through the pain of learning to walk again. . . . [He] saw a psychiatrist who helped him choose treatment options, including medication to treat his depression.

They worked together to adjust and manage his medications, talk about his problems, and help him learn how to cope with depression. . . . For Jordan, this meant learning how to have a healthy emotional balance, including being around other people and working out regularly. He is now a motivational speaker, traveling across the country and telling his story to help others. Jordan finds great satisfaction in letting youth know that they're not alone with their problems. He takes pride in helping others speak up when they need help.[8]

The forty-page booklet contains more comments from other survivors. In addition, it explains how suicide survivors can stay safe, talk to others about survival, find a counselor and support groups, take medication, and maintain a healthy lifestyle. The booklet is on the Internet and can be downloaded.

Individuals who suffer from depression should seek counseling, especially if they have thoughts of suicide or have attempted suicide. © iStock.com/AlexRaths

Sharing Stories

Dese'Rae Stage, a writer and photographer, created the website LiveThrough This.org for suicide survivors to share their stories. Des, as she calls herself, is a survivor. After attempting to kill herself, she attended suicide support meetings only to find that the groups were for people who had lost a loved one to suicide. The group did not include those who had attempted suicide. So she launched LiveThroughThis.org. Its purpose "is to show that everyone is susceptible to depression and suicidal thoughts by sharing portraits and stories of real attempt survivors—people who look just like you. . . . The fear of talking about it can be a killer." The website includes interviews of participants who agree to use their names and photos. With their interviews, they hope to raise awareness, help reduce the stigma of this health issue, and show survivors they are not alone. Each one of the interviews ends with a plea to anyone contemplating suicide to please talk to somebody. Call the National Suicide Prevention Lifeline at 800-273-8255 or online contact Lifeline Crisis Chat or Crisis Text Line.[9]

Megan Rotatori, who was a student at the University of Vermont in 2014, said in her interview that she realized she "was depressed, probably, when I was 13 or 14." She had been sexually assaulted and did not tell anyone until years later. Her depression led to self-mutilation and other self-abuse. She described her senior year in high school:

> I had gotten a lot worse with self-inflicting and self-harm and then, at that point, I was just basically spiraling out of control. I was on medication for depression, but I abused it, I don't know, just to make myself feel better. I never considered myself a drug addict, but looking back on it, that's kind of what it's about. I would just take things to try and escape when I really wasn't supposed to be taking certain things and stuff like that—mixing things—just trying to do whatever. I went through periods of drinking and smoking. . . . Then, at a certain point, I just feel like I didn't have anything left, which was obviously really hard, and that's when I ended up in the emergency room. I overdosed on my prescription meds.[10]

In 2014, Nathan Pointer, an undergraduate at Harvard University, told his story to LiveThroughThis.org. He explained that from an early age, around eight years old, he had suffered from chronic, severe depression, but his parents, teachers, and others had no clue about his condition. He covered it up, saying, "Like, if I needed to cry in the middle of the day, I would go to the bathroom and then I would do it, and then I would dilate my eyes so they wouldn't look red afterward."[11]

Pointer said, "The first time that I tried to kill myself was when I was—it was just a little bit before I turned twelve. . . . My parents didn't know, so we didn't seek any medical treatment." After his first attempt, he tried again many times. He did not confide in his parents until he was fourteen. Pointer received counseling and medication, which did not always work well. He noted,

When I was fifteen, sixteen, I had my second . . . "episode" is what I think of it as, I guess. After I came to college, I had another episode beginning. . . . Let's see. It was a little bit before I turned 20, so probably end of 2012, and it's lasted through pretty much this last year [2013]. Probably because I'm an adult, this one has had, I would say, the most tangible impact in that I'm best able to process it. . . . I came in to the school [Harvard] with this diagnosis and with this set of expectations and with a need for medication, and they got right on it. They put me in with a doctor to manage my medication and they got me into counseling . . . with a great counselor who I love to death. They have done an excellent job of serving me personally.[12]

Another participant was Niomi Provins, a student in Austin, Texas. Her interview took place in 2013 when she was nineteen. In her words,

I started thinking about suicide as an option at a very early age. I was about 12 when I first thought about it, and the first time I ever acted or anything like that, I was about 14. . . . My mother had beat the living shit out of me that day and my sisters were angry with me. My grandparents wouldn't speak to me. I didn't know where my biological father was, and my stepdad was, well, my stepdad. I really had nothing else. My family was everything to me, and I was slowly losing it. I figured nothing else would change, so I just went for it.[13]

Niomi tried a second time to kill herself when she was sixteen. She explained, "I was drinking a lot, doing a lot of drugs. I was, at that point, cutting every day just for some release of anything." She tried again the following year when she was at a friend's house, drinking and doing drugs.

I was genuinely happy. I didn't understand why I had this obscene need to just stop everything that day, because I was genuinely happy. I was with people who cared about me. In the end, I think that's why. I knew that the next day when I woke up with a hangover and I was getting sick, that my life would go back to normal—my normal—and I decided that I was going to try to drink myself until I couldn't drink anymore. My friends shoved

Depression: A Risk Factor

As survivors have underscored, depression is a major risk factor for suicide. Among those that have major depression, the risk of death by suicide is twenty times greater than for those who are not depressed. The American Association of Suicidology (AAS) lists the following signs and risk factors; in other words, a young person might be at critical risk of suicide if she or he

- Threatens to hurt or kill him- or herself, or talks of wanting to hurt or kill him- or herself
- Looks for ways to kill him- or herself by seeking access to firearms, pills, or other means
- Talks or writes about death, dying, or suicide, when these actions are out of the ordinary; if the person somehow indicates or communicates suicidal thoughts, get help immediately from a mental health professional or a professional in a hospital emergency department, or call 911[b]

The AAS website also says that if a teen shows any of the following behaviors or symptoms, that person might be in a suicidal crisis. At that point, an evaluation by a mental health professional is essential to rule out the possibility of suicide and/or to initiate appropriate treatment.

- Feelings of hopelessness
- Anxiety, agitation, trouble sleeping, or sleeping all of the time
- Expressions of having no reason for living, no sense of purpose in life
- Feelings of being trapped—like there's no way out
- Increased withdrawal from friends, family, and community
- Rage, uncontrolled anger, expressions of wanting or seeking revenge
- Reckless behavior or more risky activities, seemingly without thinking
- Dramatic mood changes
- Giving away prized possessions[c]

a plastic spoon down my throat to make sure I threw everything up so I would wake up the next day. That was the last time.[14]

Parents, teachers, and other adults in Colorado Springs, Colorado, have abundant reason to be alert for the signs of possible suicide of teenagers. "Between 2013 and 2015, 29 kids in their county had killed themselves, many from just a handful of schools," reported Max Kutner in *Newsweek*. The magazine feature described the tragic story of Riley Winters, a ninth grader at Discovery Canyon Campus High School in Colorado Springs. Her parents were divorced, and fifteen-year-old Riley alternated between her parents' homes. Kutner wrote,

> Riley was staying at her father's house one night when she downed a small bottle of whiskey, then sent out a series of troubling texts and Snapchat messages. "I'm sorry it had to be me," she wrote to one friend. Then she slipped on a blue Patagonia fleece and snuck out the basement window, carrying her father's gun.
>
> When Riley's mother and friends saw the messages, they went looking for her at local parks, gas stations and friends' houses, all the while begging her via texts and calls to come home.
>
> The next morning, they found her body in the woods behind her father's house. She'd shot herself in the head.[15]

Eunice McGarrahan, a Presbyterian pastor from Colorado Springs, wrote in late 2016, "[We have had] a rash of suicides and attempted suicides in our high school community here. But we've also had our share of other losses—one of our high schoolers just lost his dad in November and others have lost grandparents recently, so there's a lot of rawness going on."[16]

When she is called upon to counsel teenagers with their grief, McGarrahan uses the following approach, which anyone who wants to help someone deal with the death of a friend or relative can also use:

1. Just be present. Silence is okay. People should be allowed to react however they will react. This is not the time to give advice or impart understandings of the afterlife unless they ask for it. They may be silent and not show any emotional affect or they may be inconsolable. They may try to come up with explanations that may make no sense to you but don't try to correct them.
2. Don't expect a Kübler-Ross Five Stages of Grief to unfold in a linear fashion. Anger, bargaining, denial, etc. occur in unique orders and they don't always resolve neatly—as kids they are experiencing the loss on different levels.

3. Don't make false promises regarding hope or time.
4. Acknowledge that it sucks.[17]

In addition, the pastor believes "kids need to be in ongoing relationships with adults who have suffered loss and who are willing to tell their stories. This helps them understand how death fits into life. Adults need to avail themselves of training in mental health issues so that they can recognize when grieving may take a harmful turn. National Association of Mental Illness (NAMI) is a nationwide organization that hosts all sorts of seminars and training sessions that are incredibly helpful." She also says adults should "help young people learn to mourn the losses others experience, both personally and more globally (i.e., when they see the devastation of a tsunami or other disaster on the news, or what war is doing to a country). The biblical injunction to 'weep with those who weep' will help them address their own emotions when their own losses occur."[18]

The Fort Wayne, Indiana, area also saw multiple suicides in late 2016. One of the teens was a thirteen-year-old from Columbia City. Another was seventeen years of age, a third was eighteen, and a fourth was a sixteen-year-old. "Several of the victims used firearms, one chose asphyxiation," according to a news story by Brett Thomas. Jacob Becker was the sixteen-year-old. He "used a handgun to take his own life. He did it in his upstairs bedroom in the family's Kendallville [Indiana] home." His father Bob Becker told Thomas that he knew Jacob was depressed and had been bullied by classmates at East Noble High School. Jacob left a suicide note, which was published in the news story:

Hey everyone, I know a lot of people are going to end up finding this really selfish, but to be honest, I can't live like this anymore. I am tired of everything. I am tired of the way I am treated. I am tired of everything wrong I keep doing. I feel like this is best for everyone. I'm going to miss a lot of people. I am sorry everyone. Good bye. It's been a great life getting to know you all.[19]

Along with the AAS, numerous other organizations work to increase public awareness of suicide risk factors and promote scientific research on risk factors related to suicide. They also provide information for health-care providers on how to recognize depression, substance abuse, and other aspects leading to suicide. These organizations include the American Foundation for Suicide Prevention, the National Institute of Mental Health, the National Center for Injury Prevention and Control, the National Youth Violence Prevention Resource Center of the CDC, and the Substance Abuse and Mental Health Administration.

An Age-Old Issue

Since ancient times, philosophers have debated whether suicide is morally permissible. Plato and Aristotle argued against suicide, but later philosophers in ancient Greece and Rome approved of suicide to end suffering or the deterioration of old age. Early Christian philosophers opposed suicide as a violation of the commandment "thou shalt not kill," making exceptions for wars and executions. Today, most religions—Christianity, Judaism, Hinduism, Islam, and Buddhism among them—believe in the sanctity of life and condemn suicide.

Suicide Loss

No statistics are kept on how many youth and adults suffer the effects of losing a relative, friend, or classmate to suicide. Given the number of suicides, no doubt there are hundreds of thousands who mourn a suicide loss. Young children who have experienced a suicide in the family often display behavior problems, while adolescents whose family members or friends commit suicide may suffer extreme anxiety, depression, or post-traumatic stress disorder.

Families who experience suicide loss also may face ostracism or criticism because "suicide is still shrouded by stigma. Much of the general public believes that death by suicide is shameful and sinful," wrote Deborah Serani in *Psychology Today*. "Others . . . blame family members for its outcome. And then there are people who are unsure how to reach out and support those who have lost a loved one to suicide, and simply avoid the situation out of ignorance. Whatever the reason, it is important to note that the underlying structure of grief for survivors of suicide loss is intricately complicated."[20]

Discovering that a friend or relative has died by suicide is often horrifying as J. Brent Bill, a Quaker minister, wrote on Devozine.Upperoom.com. "My best friend killed himself. I found him lying on his bed with the right side of his head blown off, surrounded by a red-and-gray mess of blood and brain tissue." Brent blames himself for not seeing the signs of suicidal behavior in his friend, who talked about killing himself with a gun, drank too much, and had outbursts of rage and anxiety. "I should have gotten Greg some help or made him go to see a counselor, even if I had to drag him there. I should have gotten rid of the gun,"

Brent wrote. "After Greg's suicide, my life was a ragged mix of feelings. . . . I was confused. I spent hours trying to figure out what was so bad that he had to kill himself. It didn't make sense to me."[21]

Bill is not alone in such confusion and mixed feelings. Riley Gortsema of Grand Rapids, Michigan, attended a grief support group in 2011 to share her feelings about her brother Travis's suicide. At the time, Riley was sixteen years old and explained, "When you go through grief, your heart actually feels heavy, and your stomach feels like there's a twister in it." To relieve the pain she liked to be with friends and found it heartening when people showed they cared about Travis. "What I think makes me feel people care is when I go to Travis's grave site, and there's a worn path," she said. "People put rocks, seashells, golf balls on it."[22]

In 2015, Danielle Campoamor described on the *Huffington Post* what it is like to lose a friend to suicide. "It's hard to quantify that kind of loss or describe the unavoidable hole that's left behind." Campoamor continued,

> When you lose a friend to suicide you feel guilty. . . . So you rationalize endlessly, telling yourself that so much was out of your control and there was nothing you could have done and—in the end—it was his or her decision, but there will never be a day that doesn't pass by that you don't feel responsible. . . .
>
> When you lose a friend to suicide you hear words like "coward" and "weak" and "selfish," and the pieces of you that haven't broken yet begin to crumble. The people who didn't know him told me that what he did was wrong. They told me that he was self-centered and feeble and unworthy of the grief so many of his friends and family were feeling. They didn't understand that he felt lost . . . he felt lonely. He had a hopelessness I can't clarify. He had a mourning I couldn't possibly fathom.[23]

Help for Suicide Loss

Those who have experienced loss by suicide often seek help from online forums or join groups that meet regularly for support. These include Alliance of Hope; Parents of Suicides—Friends and Families of Suicides, a combined organization; and the American Foundation for Suicide Prevention. The latter organization sponsors an annual Survivor Day in November, when people gather to comfort each other and share stories of their loss.

Drug Overdose: Suicide or Accident?

As the number of deaths from drug overdoses increases each year, some people are questioning whether a drug overdose is intentional or accidental. In fact, Maia Szalavitz posed that question on Vice.com. It was the title of her essay: "How Many Drug Overdoses Are Actually Suicides?" She wrote,

> As a heroin addict, I saw suicidal friends overdose. In a country where ODs now kill more people than car accidents, undercounting intentional drug deaths is a risk we can't afford. When I was injecting heroin in New York in the 1980s, it was impossible not to know the risks. . . . The line between the intentional and unintentional is murky at best. Many people who truly want to live (like me, even during my active addiction) sometimes take insanely high doses and mixtures. . . .
>
> Discovering suicidal intent is of particular concern for pain patients, who are now reporting awful experiences of not being able to get needed opioids as doctors and pharmacists become more cautious and suspicious. The rate of suicide in this group is already high—and intractable pain due to denial of medication is one cause.[24]

The CDC confirms that "opioids—prescription and illicit—are the main driver of drug overdose deaths. "From 2000 to 2015 more than half a million people died from drug overdoses. 91 Americans die every day from an opioid overdose. Opioids were involved in 33,091 deaths in 2015. . . . Deaths from prescription opioids—drugs like oxycodone, hydrocodone, and methadone—have more than quadrupled since 1999," the CDC reported.[25] "Significant increases in drug overdose death rates from 2014 to 2015 were primarily seen in the Northeast and South Census Regions. States with statistically significant increases in drug overdose death rates from 2014 to 2015 included Connecticut, Florida, Illinois, Kentucky, Louisiana, Maine, Maryland, Massachusetts, Michigan, New Hampshire, New Jersey, New York, North Carolina, Ohio, Pennsylvania, Rhode Island, Tennessee, Washington, and West Virginia," according to the CDC.[26]

As of December 2016, the CDC had not listed California as having significant increases in drug overdose deaths, but the problem persists in the state. In Ventura County heroin killed thirty-three people in 2015, "with 12 deaths in the city of Ventura alone," the *Ventura County Star* reported. "The frequency of deaths in the county, according to nine years of data from the California Department of Public Health, has consistently surpassed the fatality rate across California. Many observers link the heroin problem to the county and nationwide epidemic of painkiller abuse, contending that people who are addicted to prescription meds eventually turn to heroin."[27] The newspaper did not report whether the deadly overdoses in Ventura County were linked to suicide or were unintentional.

Suicides in Military Families

You have probably read or heard about active duty military members or veterans with post-traumatic stress disorder (PTSD) who have attempted suicide or have died by their own hand. The U.S. Department of Veterans Affairs (VA) explains, "Many Veterans have very disturbing thoughts and extreme guilt about actions taken during times of war. These thoughts can often overwhelm the Veteran and make it hard for him or her to deal with the intense feelings."[28] An average of twenty veterans died from suicide each day in 2014, totaling more than seven thousand annually. Eighteen percent of all suicides in the United States were veterans.[29]

The VA established the Veterans Crisis Line in 2007 as one measure to prevent suicide. The suicide prevention line is also called the Military Crisis Line for active service members as well as those in the National Guard and Reserve. The crisis line can be reached by calling 800-273-8255 or sending a text to 838255. Responders, who receive intensive training in suicide prevention and crisis inter-

Many members of the military who have been in combat suffer from post-traumatic stress disorder. Unless treated, they may consider suicide. © iStock.com/Filjka

vention, answer the calls and texts and dispatch emergency services when there is imminent suicidal crisis.

Often overlooked in the military are suicidal children and spouses of armed service members. A major feature by CNN titled "The Uncounted" included the story of a suicidal teenager, Kristi Anne Raspperry, and her mother, Heather Moates, who also had been suicidal. In 2010, Heather was caring for her military husband John, who had PTSD. Overcome by John's violent behavior, Heather tried to kill herself but did not reveal that attempted suicide to her daughter.

In 2014, nineteen-year-old Kristi was living with her parents outside Savannah, Georgia, and CNN's Ashley Fantz interviewed Kristi about her attempted suicide. Kristi explained,

> I was around 11 or 12 when my dad deployed. I was very sad because my dad was going, possibly, to die and it was just, I didn't know what was going to happen to him.
>
> I always kind of grew up in the military brat life, so I knew that sometimes when your parents deploy, sometimes they don't come back. . . .
>
> I talked to a few of my friends whose parents had also deployed at the time so they were always there for me.[30]

Kristi said that when her father "came home the first time, I did notice there was something kind of off about him. He was a lot more aggressive, and he didn't laugh as much as he usually did. He didn't really trust people. . . . Any loud noises, he would immediately find where it was coming from. At the time, I had no idea what PTSD was. . . . He wasn't my dad; he was some monster that took his place."[31]

During the interview, Kristi explained that her father and mother once got in a "serious fight," and she had to call 911. "I'm not really sure what happened after that because I kind of blanked it out from my memories because it was a bit too much. All I remember is the police took him away." From then on, Kristi became seriously depressed and thought about suicide, "just like end everything. Just, like, if life's this bad, maybe, you know, death, that would make everything better for me." Fortunately, Kristi talked to her mother, who shared her experience and hospitalization for attempted suicide. With her mother's help, Kristi found a counselor and began getting psychological help.[32]

FUNERALS, BURIALS, AND MEMORIALS

"She was a beautiful soul. . . . I called her my cupcake because she was so cute and sweet."—part of a eulogy for Sabrina Dolling's deceased little sister[1]

Funerals and burial rituals help survivors of the deceased—family, friends, coworkers, classmates, and others—face the reality of death and mourn. Religious and cultural factors help determine whether the funeral will be elaborate or simple, public or private, religious or secular, and where it will be held. These factors also influence whether the dead body will be present at a service, if there will be a viewing or visitation, and if so, whether there will be a casket and whether the remains will be buried or cremated. One common funeral ritual includes taking the body to a funeral home where a mortician prepares the deceased for burial or entombment. At the funeral home, mourners can pay their respects to the family and honor the deceased before a hearse carries the body to a cemetery.

Funerals usually involve some type of ceremony, formal or informal, either steeped in long-held customs or specially created for the deceased and his or her loved ones. Gifts of flowers or monetary donations to charities are frequently part of funerals as are food and drink following burials. Funeral ceremonies often include readings, blessings, music, and eulogies (tributes) to the deceased.

Unfortunately, in many cases in recent years, funerals have been conducted for teenagers who have died due to tragic circumstances. One such funeral in June 2016 was held in Holland, Michigan, for a sixteen-year-old Holland Christian High School student, Riley Hoeksema. He and his teenage friend Levi Winkle were in an inflatable boat on Lake Michigan. The boat capsized and a passerby was able to save Levi, but Riley drowned. After Riley's body was recovered, his family held a funeral attended by relatives and numerous classmates, among them Levi. At the funeral Levi spoke about his friend. As reported by

A Funeral Cortege

A funeral cortege is a procession of mourners traveling to a burial site. It has been part of funeral and burial practices since ancient times. After a traditional funeral in the United States, the cortege begins with an escort car equipped with a flashing or emergency light, which leads the procession. Other vehicles that are part of the procession follow with clergy and casket bearers, then the hearse, and cars with the deceased's family and friends. However, the order of the cortege may vary, depending on the wishes of the deceased's family. Processions for firefighters, police officers, and numerous government officials may also include special vehicles such as fire engines and trucks, motorcycles, and caissons (open, horse-drawn wagons that hold the deceased).

A funeral cortege has the right-of-way along a roadway, and it is illegal to disrupt or drive through a funeral procession, providing the vehicles are conspicuously marked with funeral flags or windshield signage and have their headlights or hazard flasher lights on. When a head of state or a famous person dies, the route of the funeral cortege is generally publicized so that mourners can pay their respects as the procession moves by.

Channel 8 TV, Levi said, "Riley, I'm going to miss you. We went through a lot together and I can only imagine what we still had coming. . . . You're already experiencing the greatest adventure, and I'm sure you will have plenty to show me when I catch up."[2]

Another tragic death of a teenager in 2016 brought mourners to a wake and funeral for Dayshen McKenzie held at a Staten Island, New York, funeral home. Dayshen was sixteen and reportedly was running away from either "a racist mob" or a "gang," depending on who told the story. While fleeing, he had an extreme asthma attack and died. According to Joseph Stepansky of the *New York Daily News*, Dayshen's friends attended the funeral and as a tribute wore shirts inscribed with "RIP Poppa," Dayshen's nickname. A classmate, Jaydah Flack, told Stepansky, "Poppa was the bro, we knew each other for mad long. . . . He was a fun person, he always made it fun. There was nothing but good vibes. He was a good person, we love Poppa."[3]

Eulogies

Eulogies at funerals may be presented by family members, friends, clergy, or the mortician. Unless some religions require clergy to present the eulogy, which often involves a sermon, there is no right or wrong way to deliver a tribute. Countless examples of suggested eulogies and how to present them are available on the Internet and in books, as well as from funeral directors. Eulogies or tributes may be biographical sketches of a deceased family member, friend, classmate, or coworker. Perhaps some of the most difficult eulogies to present are those for someone who has died of a drug overdose, suicide, or murder.

Some eulogies are made up of numerous quotes that mirror a person's life. Or a eulogy could be a poem. It can also be humorous, especially if the deceased person was known as a comedian or a mischief maker. For the most part, eulogies are heartfelt remembrances of loved ones.

On Write-Out-Loud.com, Sabrina Dolling of California wrote a eulogy for her little sister Jessica, whom she called "a beautiful soul. . . . I called her my cupcake because she was so cute and sweet, and she in turn called me her sugar momma because I always spoiled her and did my best to take care of her." Sabrina ended her eulogy with this advice for others who are mourning a death: "I will leave you with this last thought. Tell people you love them more times than you think they should hear it, especially if you think they already know. I never got to tell Jessica just how important she was to me, although I know in my heart she felt it."[4]

Eulogy for Mom

As an example of paying tribute, I include an edited portion of the eulogy I wrote for my mother's memorial service:

Lots of people called her "mom." But her given name was Beatrice or Bea, who early in her life, tried to express her creative spirit in paintings. She wanted to attend the Art Institute in Chicago for training. But her father would have none of that! Girls didn't need to be doing such silly things and it probably was a "sinful" undertaking. Besides, all hands were needed on the farm.

Mom's creativity was channeled in other ways, appearing in such practical skills as cooking, baking, sewing, quilting, embroidering, and "saving for a rainy day." Saving was a passion with mom. . . . She saved egg shells to be buried in the garden to enrich the soil. Egg cartons were saved for reuse. . . . Glass jars and bottles were saved for preserving: tomatoes, pickles, peaches, apricots, grape juice, tomato juice, jellies.

Anyone need a rubber band? You were bound to find one on the broom closet door knob. Mom saved hundreds of scraps of cloth that might be used for a quilt or for patching clothes. Thin or ripped bed sheets were patched with flour or sugar sack material. One infamous sheet that I recall had at least six such patches. Worn blankets were sewn together to create a new-used bed covering.

Every bit of paper with a blank side was saved for writing on again. Greeting cards, birth and death announcements, shower and wedding invitations, letters, and countless other written communications were saved to reread dozens of times. Mementoes and photographs from all types of events were never thrown away. Neither were paper bags, string, pencil stubs, and countless other everyday items that someone might be able to reuse someday. . . .

I think of Mom hemming skirts and dresses and fitting my brothers with pants and suits she made on her trusty Singer; pouring boiling water over lemons and honey to soothe our sore throats; showing me how to iron men's shirts the "professional" and "efficient" way; insisting that Saturday was not for lolling around in bed—there were household chores to do; Mom dressing for some event, always meticulous with her hair, hat, stylish dress and shoes—and gloves. Don't forget the gloves, a pair for every occasion. Mom fussing, planning, organizing, and preparing for weddings, births, funerals, charity events, family gatherings. . . .

Mom died at the age of 97. Peace to thee, the preacher said.

Funeral Practices

Funeral practices vary with ethnic and religious groups. They can range from a quiet family gathering at a grave site to a detailed observance in a place of worship to a week-long event, or even a jazz commemoration. In the United States, one of the most boisterous funeral processions is the New Orleans jazz-tinged funeral procession. It expresses both joy and grief as a marching band leads mourners to a burial plot for the deceased. At first the band plays dirges, but once the body is buried, the music is upbeat and lively.

Most U.S. funerals, however, are based on religious beliefs. Traditional funerals are usually conducted by clergy in a church or chapel setting with prayers, hymns, eulogies, and frequently a sermon. Viewing the body may also be part of the funeral service. At the end of the funeral, the casket is usually carried out of the room by pallbearers, placed in a hearse, and taken to the cemetery. Family members and others follow to participate in a final graveside ceremony.

A religious funeral in a Baptist church was held for Akyra Murray, who was eighteen years old and the youngest of the forty-nine people killed at the Pulse nightclub in Orlando, Florida, on June 12, 2016. The service for Murray was held at Monument Baptist Church in West Philadelphia, Pennsylvania. Murray was a graduate of West Catholic Prep School, and had a basketball scholarship to attend Mercyhurst University, a Catholic liberal arts college in Erie, Pennsylvania. "In high school, she was a 1,000-point scorer and ranked third in her class," according to the *Daily Mail*. At the four-hour service, a four-piece band played softly and mourners filed past Murray's open casket. One of the mourners, twenty-year-old Patience Carter, a survivor of the Pulse killings and friend of Akyra, told a *Daily Mail* reporter that Akyra would always be remembered. "If I got to get up every day and run up and down these streets, and say Akyra Murray 342 million times to let them know who you are and what you've done."[5]

If you ever plan to attend a funeral in which the religious practices are unfamiliar, it can be helpful and save you from embarrassment to know some of the varied customs. For example, at some funerals, it is insulting to mourners if you wear flip-flops. Or it may be mandatory to wear a black dress for females, a black suit for males. A head covering may also be required, depending on the religious practices.

Funeral rites for Roman Catholics include a vigil (or wake as it's commonly known), a funeral mass, and burial in a Catholic cemetery. The vigil is the initial rite following death and before the funeral liturgy. The wake usually takes place in a funeral home, family home, or parish church.

One example of a funeral mass with Monsignor Thomas Fryar attending was held for teenager Patric Lantz at St. Thomas More Catholic Church in Centennial, Colorado, on January 26, 2016. Patric and two other teenagers had fallen through an icy retention pond on January 14, 2016, and Patric drowned. One of the other teens, Max Gantnier, was in critical condition after the fall and died days later.

Half of the church was filled with Patric's classmates and rugby teammates. Eighteen-year-old Braeden Evert, who trained Patric on the high school's rugby team, told the *Denver Post* that Patric "will forever be my brother. . . . It was such an honor just to know him."[6]

The traditional Jewish funeral is usually brief, held as quickly as possible after death. Before the burial, there is no wake or visitation period since viewing the body is considered disrespectful. A long-established custom is for relatives of the deceased to tear their clothing as a sign of loss. This practice, however, is not part of Reform Judaism. Reform Jews usually wear torn black ribbons given to them by the rabbi. At an Orthodox Jewish funeral service, men and women sit in separate sections. Men wear yarmulkes or skullcaps, and women may be expected to cover their heads with a hat, scarf, or piece of lace. The service itself includes reading of Psalms, a eulogy, and memorial prayer.

A Muslim funeral is held no longer than twenty-four hours after a person's death, so embalming is not necessary. Members of the deceased's family or the Islamic community wash the body of the deceased in a prescribed ritual. "Preparing the body for burial is a Fard Kifaayah—communal obligation on Muslims. Washing the dead body prior to shrouding and burial is obligatory, according to numerous recorded instructions," states Bilal Abu Aisha on MissionIslam.com. "As a general rule, males should take the responsibility of washing males, and females should wash females. The only exception to this rule is in the case of husband and wife, or small children." The body is then wrapped in a clean, white

The stones on a Jewish tombstone are signs that people have visited the grave and commemorated the deceased. © *iStock.com/JRLPhotographer*

shroud (called the kafan), usually two or three sheets. Then a congregational prayer service called the Janazah is held, after which the body is buried.[7]

In a 2013 article for the *Guardian*, a Muslim woman explained how she and her two sisters prepared the body of Umma, as they called their mother, who was from Bangladesh. Momtaz Begum-Hossain wrote,

> In Islam it is a daughter's duty to wash her mother and prepare her for the afterlife. . . . Umma was so devoted to her religion that I sensed she would be proud her daughters were taking part in such a symbolic ritual. As her limbs were lifted and we took it in turns to scrub her, it seemed as if her expressions were changing. She was a puppet, being moved, bent over, turned from side to side. I didn't know it was possible to get this close to a dead person, let alone share in the most intimate experience their body would ever go through. . . . Afterwards she was dried with towels and scented with rose water. . . . Umma's hair was combed and plaited and her body wrapped in the white fabric that Ubba, my father, had brought back from Mecca.[8]

Begum-Hossain ended her article with these words: "I reminisce over it all as a special memory. Not everyone has a chance to say goodbye properly to someone they love, but I did more than that."[9]

In Islamic practice, only men are allowed to escort the body to a burial site. © *iStock.com/ mirzavis*

> ### ⚠ Now You Know
>
> During the 1800s in the United States, it was customary to send elaborate funeral cards to inform family members and others in the community of the date, time, and place of the funeral. The cards were about the size of a postcard and made of heavy cardboard. They might be bordered in black or have embossed letters and symbols of mourning such as weeping willows or sheaves of wheat. Or there were images of the Grim Reaper, an hourglass, or crossed bones. While such cards are no longer used, leaflets, bookmarks, or folded booklets are given out at funerals to memorialize the deceased.

Native American Death Ceremonies

Native American tribes conduct a wide variety of death ceremonies, such as those for the Kiowa, Comanche, Kaw, and Lakota, to name a few. Toby Blackstar of the Kiowa tribe in Oklahoma is a Native American funeral director and described funeral customs in his community. In a podcast, Steve Turner interviewed Blackstar, who represents the Kiowa and Comanche tribes and the Comanche Nation Funeral Home in Lawton, Oklahoma. Turner asked Blackstar whether Native Americans currently follow the same death rituals as their ancestors did. Blackstar responded,

> I do find this to be true and I'll be giving you aspects from both the Kiowa death ceremonials and Comanche death ceremonials. We have our own funeral home and when you work with a member of a Native American culture there are a lot of traditions that must happen. For example there is a cedar or smoke that is tethered upon the body for a blessing and a prayer to the body that is now taking off to what they call "their journey." The "cedar or smoke ceremony" is for the members that have been left behind so they don't take the death too hard. Now, the Kiowa are more prone to have Christian burials that have been taught by the missionaries of long ago.[10]

Blackstar went on to explain customs of other tribes—the Otoe-Missouria of North Oklahoma in Ponca City and the Kaw, the Osage, and the Ponca tribal communities in Oklahoma.

> Their practices are that the body is taken to the home, a church or a cultural centre. If somebody were to die this morning, we would take the

body to the prep room to prepare the body. They would come to the funeral home to make the arrangements and on the fourth day from the time of death . . . they would feed the body at different times. They have cooks that made breakfast, lunch and supper. These things are things . . . that they recommend for the soul . . . and the body to continue to be nourished. The belief is when that soul leaves the body on the day of death, that soul wanders wherever family members may live, whether it be in Oklahoma, Ohio, Georgia etc. Wherever there are family members, that loved one will actually go and visit them before they make their journey up to the heavens and they take four days to do so.[11]

On the Pine Ridge Reservation, the Lakota (Sioux) "blend old and new traditions. Funeral practices incorporate Native American spirituality and Christian sentiment, so families invite both clergy and medicine men to lead services," according to Danie Koskan, a correspondent for the *Rapid City Journal*. He spoke to Pat Janis, who "oversees the Oglala Sioux Tribe's Burial Assistance Program. As director, he determines who qualifies for a tribal burial and how much of the bill will be covered." In his article, Koskan wrote,

Wakes typically occur in large public spaces on the reservation. Meeting halls and school gymnasiums are common indoor sites, but not all wakes occur within four walls. Two Dogs, a medicine man, recalls a summertime wake or two in which the body was placed in a teepee.

Wake and funeral ceremonies tend to be held in the same location. Once a body arrives, it isn't moved until it's taken to its final resting place.[12]

A Christian minister may take part in a funeral service, and following the minister's portion, a Lakota ceremony begins:

A medicine man offers prayers, and Lakota songs are sung, often to the beat of a drum group. Toward the end of the traditional rites, guests are invited to view the body one last time. One by one, those in attendance pass by the casket, paying their respects to the deceased and offering their condolences to those left behind.

Well-wishers leave "spiritual food," otherwise known as wasna or pemmican. This traditional Lakota recipe of dried buffalo, fat and berries forms a cake that's ideal for traveling. "We believe the spirit will journey for four days after they are put into the ground," Two Dogs said. Gifts placed in the casket are equally ideal for the journey ahead. Traditional Native American beliefs hold that death is not an end.[13]

Burial Mounds

The indigenous people of North America built numerous burial mounds across the United States, and archaeologists continue to find new and different mounds throughout the nation. Some have been designated as state or national historic sites and are listed in the National Register of Historic Places. Others are protected by private citizens who have discovered the mounds on their lands.

Burial mounds are hill-like structures of dirt, shells, stones, sand, or other earthen materials. Over the years, native burial mounds have been desecrated by people digging for artifacts and by archeological teams and construction and road-building companies. The Native American Graves Protection and Repatriation Act of 1990 was passed to protect Native American graves and related items, and to control their removal. The act requires federal agencies to consult appropriate tribes or Native Hawaiian groups when they encounter such sites, either in the course of planned excavations or through inadvertent discovery. Indigenous people determine the appropriate treatment of human remains and cultural objects. Many states also have passed legislation that addresses the discovery and disposition of graves.

One example is the Grave Creek Mound Historic Site in Moundsville, West Virginia, just south of Wheeling. It was built between 250 and 150 BCE by the Adena, the people responsible for the beginning of mound building cultures. The Grave Creek Mound is the largest conical-shaped burial mound in the United States and originally stood about 70 feet tall but is now 62 feet high and 240 feet in diameter, containing approximately fifty-seven thousand tons of dirt. The first mound was built to hold the remains of a great warrior, chief, religious leader, or other important person.

Dozens of other conical mounds exist in West Virginia. The Criel Mound, which was probably built between 250 and 150 BCE, is 35 feet high and 175 feet in diameter and is exceeded in size only by the Grave Creek Mound, according to the West Virginia Division of Culture and History.[a]

Alternative Funerals

An increasing number of Americans are forgoing traditional funeral rituals and opting for alternative ways to commemorate the deceased. Some alternative funerals are planned by environmentalists who are concerned about the possible destructive effects of the chemicals used in the embalming process and the use of potentially harmful materials in coffins. Others may simply want a secular and more natural funeral and burial in an area such as a woodland.

Some people opt for an alternative funeral because they want to bypass funeral homes and the services of undertakers. Or they choose the alternative funeral because they want a more intimate and personal service and one less costly than a traditional funeral. It is also an opportunity for people to record what they believe is the essence of their life, and to make statements about what they feel they have contributed to society.

In some cases, people who opt for alternative funerals may mix rituals from various cultures such as Buddhist, indigenous, and Egyptian rites. Some make arrangements for burials at sea. Others have signed up with organizations that will mummify their bodies. One such group in Salt Lake City is called Some Mum, which has not yet mummified any human bodies but has preserved numerous pets.

An alternative funeral may also include a ceremony at home with the deceased placed in a simple casket (often one made of cardboard or pine) and close relatives and friends gathering for a service. A home funeral was common a century ago when people died at home and family members prepared the body for viewing and burial. This practice is still maintained by some religious and ethnic groups, but with most Americans dying in hospitals and other impersonal institutions, they generally have turned to the funeral industry to care for their dead. Nevertheless the growing movement to care for one's own dead has focused on home funerals and burials.

Contrary to popular belief and the erroneous claims of some funeral directors, most states allow home burials, although they may be limited by local zoning regulations. In rural areas, for example, home burial may be permitted as long as various conditions are met, such as the required depth of the grave and specified distance from underground water sources.

For home burials, caskets do not have to be purchased from a mortuary, as many people believe. Some casket companies now sell directly to consumers, or caskets can be ordered from companies advertising on the Internet. People who have carpentry skills may make coffins in which to bury their loved ones.

For example, after the death of their one-month-old son, the parents took care of the infant's body themselves. They wanted to bury their child on their own land, but that meant completing a lot of paperwork. So they opted to have their son cremated. However, the father's first step was to build a simple, small coffin. He lined the box with beach sand, grass, and flowers and put a stuffed lamb inside. Then the father painted a tugboat on the front of it, because his son had always reminded him of a tugboat—"a little guy who was tough and stubborn, and cute," he told a National Public Radio reporter.[14]

Another form of alternative funeral for a deceased person whose body has been cremated is spreading the ashes in a favorite place. For example, a family may travel to a lake, mountaintop, golf course, or even a historic site as a burial place for the ashes. Or they sprinkle the ashes among backyard plants, flowers, trees, or other growing things. Family or friends of the person who has died may plant a tree or bush and include cremated remains in the soil.

Internet websites, books, and magazine articles discuss how alternative funerals can be arranged. Yet they are not for everyone, especially those who are not comfortable even talking about death let alone their own mortality.

Military Funerals

Over the past decades, many active members of the U.S. Armed Forces have died in foreign wars. When military men and women are killed in combat, their bodies are transferred in a solemn and dignified manner to the United States. Remains are transported by military cargo plane to the Dover Air Force Base in Dover, Delaware. There a hearse carries the remains to the Air Force Mortuary Affairs Operations center, where the body is prepared for burial, outfitted in a full-dress uniform, and placed in a casket covered with the American flag.

Military funerals and burial services are perhaps some of the most traditional in the United States, although many of the customs stem from British practices. If requested by the family, military funerals are provided for deceased members of the active armed services and eligible veterans. The U.S. Department of Defense (DoD) is responsible for the military funeral honors ceremony, and the Department of Veterans Affairs (VA) National Cemetery Administration staff assists with military funeral honors at VA national cemeteries.

Although military funerals have a long tradition, in 2001 the DoD began a program called Honoring Those Who Served, which governs funeral honors for eligible veterans. The law requires that every eligible veteran receive a military funeral honors ceremony if the family requests it. At least two members of the honors detail for a veteran's funeral must be members of the armed forces; one of the honors detail must be a member of the branch of service of which the veteran was a member. The remainder of the detail can consist of members of the armed forces or members of VA organizations or others approved under regulations prescribed by the secretary of defense. The VA provides U.S. flags for funerals of military veterans. If a service member dies while on active duty, the flag is provided by the deceased's branch of service.

At the funeral ceremony, a U.S. flag is draped over the closed casket with the blue field of stars placed at the top left portion of the casket. If the casket is open, the flag is folded in a triangle and placed in the casket above the left shoulder of the deceased.

Before burial, the flag is removed from a closed casket and folded in a traditional triangle. The flag is folded thirteen times, representing the original thirteen colonies and represents the tri-cornered hat worn by the Patriots of the American Revolution. When folded, no red or white stripe should be evident, leaving only the blue field with stars. (Directions for folding the flag in a precise manner are shown on the VA website, http://www.vba.va.gov/pubs/forms/VBA-27-2008 -ARE.pdf.) At the end of a funeral, the flag is presented to the next of kin, or if none is present, the flag may be presented to a close friend or associate on request.

At full military funerals, officers are entitled to the use of the caisson. The horses and riders of the U.S. Army Caisson Platoon participate in numerous historic parades and ceremonies, but the platoon's primary mission is to escort funeral services at Arlington National Cemetery. Caisson horses, which are donated or purchased from ranches throughout the United States, must be black, gray, or white and are housed in stables at Fort Myer, Virginia. The horses require extensive training, which is conducted by members of the elite Caisson Platoon who have also undergone rigorous schooling. Soldiers not only care for the horses but also learn to ride at erect military attention in a military forward position.

A riderless horse may accompany the procession in funerals for U.S. Army and Marine Corps officers with the rank of colonel and above. Cannon salutes may also be part of the ceremony for officers. A four-star general may receive a seventeen-gun salute; three-star general receives fifteen. A two-star and one-star general receive thirteen and eleven salutes, respectively. The president of the United States is entitled to a twenty-one-gun salute, while other high state officials receive nineteen guns.

Homeless Veterans

When veterans are homeless and die, they, too, may receive a military funeral—if someone cares enough to make it happen. At the University of Detroit Jesuit High School and Academy, six students took part in a special program to pay final tribute to deceased homeless veterans. The program began in October 2015 with students volunteering to serve as pallbearers at the funerals of three unclaimed, homeless veterans. (On January 1, 2014, there were nearly fifty thousand homeless vets in the United States.) In the ceremonies, caskets were covered with the American flag and the pathway to the cemetery was lined with people holding flags.

In a story about the student program first published on October 26, 2015, on *Today* (and republished in November 2015), Terri Peters reported these comments from students:

"I am so glad I was able to help out those three brave men, giving them a proper celebration of the life they led," said Michael O'Connor, one of the students. "I did not know these men, but being able to show them respect was important to me."

"I felt it was a real privilege to be a part of this service for these men who have fought for our country. Although none of us knew them, I felt honored to be a part of the service," said Leonard Froehlich, a high school senior. "Above all, we gave these men a truly dignified funeral."

Nick Benedetto, 17, a senior at the school, said he's done a great deal of reflection on his experience as a pallbearer. "I know that these people had loved ones and, whether or not these loved ones could be there to say goodbye, it does not change the fact that everyone deserves a proper burial. . . . I realized that none of us present knew anything about the deceased. However, we were all there to pay them respect for serving our country. After that, I felt a sense of peace and was thankful that I was able to be a part of the services."[15]

Teens Play Taps at Veterans' Funerals

An Illinois law that became effective January 1, 2017, allows high school buglers to be excused from school to play Taps at funerals for veterans. "Illinois is believed to be the fifth state to have such a law," according to a *Chicago Tribune* report. Between 2014 and 2016, Jack Bumann of Woodhill, Illinois, was one of the buglers. He is a member of the Youth Trumpet and Taps Corp that honors veterans at funerals.

In 2016, Bumann was a senior at Alwood High School and told reporter Joan Cary, "'When they call me, I go. . . . Whenever they need me, I'm waiting.' He added that he and other student trumpet players are 'trying to honor the people who fought for our country.'"[16]

Another member of the Taps Corp is sixteen-year-old Andrew Hunter of Batavia, Illinois. "He plays trumpet at Batavia High School, and with the help of his band director, learned taps so he could join the group," Cary reported, adding, "Though the new Illinois law pertains to students as young as 6th-graders, musicians have to be in high school to qualify for the Youth Trumpet & Taps Corps. They also must complete online training and submit video auditions or audition before their school band director."[17]

CULTURAL AND RELIGIOUS BELIEFS ABOUT DEATH

"We celebrate life, and commemorate death, in a way that is never separated from religion."—Veronica Mena of El Salvador[1]

Just as funerals, burial rituals, and memorials are influenced by cultural and religious traditions, so are beliefs about death and bereavement. These differences are important to recognize should you want to comfort a grieving friend or relative whose faith is different from your own. Or perhaps you just want to understand religious customs or cultural ceremonies observed when someone dies. Learning about cultural beliefs about death may provide some insight on the diversity of attitudes and viewpoints regarding life and death.

Cultural Beliefs

Depending on their culture and heritage, people perceive death and dying in diverse ways. A young Hispanic woman explained her beliefs this way:

In my Hispanic culture we celebrate life, and commemorate death, in a way that is never separated from religion. For many of us, being aware of why we do this is not as important as following the inherited traditions and customs. But taking the time to learn why helps faith go deeper. . . . I will share how we celebrate someone's passing from this life to the next. . . .

The pastor of my local parish recently attended a funeral in my hometown of Charlotte [North Carolina]; but he didn't find the solemn atmosphere that he is accustomed to seeing at funerals. He was almost shocked to find a *mariachi* band singing a last farewell to the beloved departed.

Somebody's grandmother had died, he told me, and she was dressed as a queen, with a gown and tiara.

This is another important part of my Hispanic culture: when a loved one dies, some families decide to offer *el último adiós* (the last farewell) with *mariachis*! Some people even asked for it as part of their will. It is also common to bring *mariachis* to the cemetery for *Día de los Muertos* (Day of the Dead) to remember the faithful departed with joy, and singing songs such as "*Cuando muera no me lloren*" (When I die, do not cry for me).[2]

In Hawaii, which may be the most multicultural U.S. state (New Yorkers might disagree), the cultures "blend with each other, and values, beliefs and customs blend as well. However, traditional death attitudes and customs are kept," wrote Panagiotis Pentaris, whose research on culture and death appeared on Academia. edu in 2010. He explained that death and the grief process proceed at their "own pace and no one can hurry that," adding, "Nowadays, Native Hawaiians strongly believe that a death of one person connects that person to the family members who have died in the past. Death for the Native Hawaiians has become a way for the deceased to move to a higher level after earth and thus Native Hawaiians do not mourn death."[3]

Religious Beliefs

Covering every religious belief about death would require an encyclopedic publication, but several are covered in subsequent sections.

Christianity

Christian beliefs are probably the most familiar. However, there are three broad Christian groups—Catholic, Eastern Orthodox, and Protestant—and among Protestants there are numerous denominations. Their basic principles derive from the biblical New Testament. Christians believe in the trinity of God: the Father, the Son, and the Holy Spirit. According to the belief, Jesus is the Son of God, who was born on earth, crucified, resurrected, and rose to heaven. Christians pray in Jesus's name, ask for forgiveness of sins, and expect to be rewarded with eternal life in heaven.

Some Christians also believe in faith healing and refuse medical care because they believe that prayer is the only way to heal the sick. In fact, the parents of Canadian teenager Alex Radita, who had been diagnosed at age three with type 1 diabetes, which is fatal if not treated with insulin, firmly believed that their fifteen-year-old son was not ill. The parents, Emil and Rodica Radita, adamantly denied that Alex had a treatable disease. They simply did not believe the medical diagnosis. And Alex wasted away. In 2013, Alex "died at age 15, weighing only 37 pounds," according to several news reports.[4]

Judaism

The basic principles of Judaism were spelled out in the twelfth century by Rabbi Moshe ben Maimon, who was known as Rambam. These basic principles cover many pages in his *Book of Knowledge*, but are condensed here:

1. God exists, "a Being who is complete in every manner of existence."
2. God is "One and a Unity unlike any other unity."
3. God is incorporeal—"this One is not a physical body and not a force in a body, and not subject to things that affect bodies."
4. "God is Primordial, namely that this One was the absolute First."
5. Prayer is to be directed to God alone and to no other.
6. The words of the prophets are true.
7. Moses was the greatest of the prophets and his words are true.
8. The Written Torah (first 5 books of the Bible) and Oral Torah (teachings now contained in the Talmud and other writings) were given to Moses.
9. There will be no other Torah.[5]

Teenager Nora, whose interfaith family is Jewish and Catholic, was profiled in *I Believe in . . . Christian, Jewish, Muslim Young People Speak about Their Faith*. She noted, "There is one very large issue, obviously, that Jews and Christians differ on, which is Jesus and the Holy Trinity. . . . But what I've learned . . . is Judaism and Catholicism are really similar in many ways. So much of Catholicism is taken from Judaism. I'll go to synagogue and we'll be reading things, and I'll be like, 'we just sang that in a song on Sunday.'"[6]

Islam

For Muslims, death is like a trip from one world to another. "Ideally, the dying person will have asked for God's forgiveness, prepared a will, performed the ritual full-body ablution before prayer, and recited the *shahadah* (profession of faith) before their death." Upon death, the deceased person's body is washed and covered in a white shroud "consisting of three pieces of clean, white cloth that contain no sewn seams or knots," and buried as soon as possible, according to Professor Amir Hussain, theological studies, Loyola Marymount University in Los Angeles.[7]

In the Islamic belief, death is not the end of life but rather a time of transition. While on earth, a Muslim's duty is to prepare for the afterlife by practicing the five pillars of Islam:

1. Shahada—declaring or expressing fundamental Islamic belief
2. Salat—praying five times daily
3. Zakat—giving alms or donations to charities
4. Saum—fasting during Ramadan
5. Hajj—making a pilgrimage to Mecca, if able[8]

Did You Know?

An ancient religion called Zoroastrianism was the basis of "Jewish, Christian and Muslim beliefs concerning God and Satan, the soul, heaven and hell, the virgin birth of the savior, the slaughter of the innocents, resurrection, the final judgment, etc.," according to Religious Tolerance of Ontario, Canada. "The religion was founded by Zarathushtra (also known as Zoroaster) in Persia, which is modern-day Iran. It may have been the world's first monotheistic faith."[a]

Zoroasterism

Zoroasterism still survives with a small group of worshippers in India called the Parsees. Their beliefs about death differ from those of the Jewish, Christian, and Muslim faiths. According to Zoroastrianism, immediately after the body dies, it becomes impure. "Contaminating the elements (Earth, Air, Fire and Water) with decaying matter such as a corpse is considered sacrilege," according to a report in the *Guardian*, so Zoroastrians build outdoor platforms for their dead. In Mumbai, where many Zoroastrians live, they traditionally place a dead body on a "(dokhma or 'Tower of Silence') to be exposed to the sun and eaten by birds of prey such as vultures." However, the practice may end because of changing times in India. Zoroastrians are now likely to cremate their dead as their fellow believers do in other countries.[b]

Buddhism

Buddhists, as well as members of some other Asian religions, believe that life in the present world is, for the most part, a time of suffering, but people are reincarnated—or reborn again and again—in order to be released from a constant cycle, known as the law of karma. Under this impersonal law, an individual's deeds—good or bad—determine rewards or punishments in each successive life. In other words, one reaps what she or he sows.

Ultimately, Buddhists hope to achieve nirvana, a state in which a person is liberated from desire—that is, wanting and craving worldly things. In the Buddhist view, after death the spirit of the deceased goes through a process called bardos that includes first the recognition that one has died and second the experience of sensations felt during a lifetime because of one's karma. At the end of the process, a highly developed person who has no more cravings enters Nirvana because there is no reason to be reborn. Reincarnation is required for those who are not yet liberated.[9]

Dharmachari Vishvapani of London said he "became a Buddhist at the age of fifteen." He explained in an essay,

> My family weren't Buddhist, they were Jewish, and I had had a Jewish upbringing. It is not that I disliked Judaism, but when I got to my teenage years I started to ask questions. I wanted to know if the Bible stories were really true when they differed from the versions of history and science I was learning at school. I started to read more serious books than I had looked at till then and realised that there were many different ways of understanding the world. What if there was no God? And if there wasn't, was there a difference between right and wrong, or was it just a matter of opinion?[10]

Vishvapani was introduced to the religion by his older sister, a Buddhist. "I'd heard only a little about Buddhism before that and I had the idea that it was something weird and foreign," he noted. But he began to attend a community of Buddhists, and he eventually became a member of the Friends of the Western Buddhist Order, now called the Cambridge Buddhist Centre. Vishvapani explained that he posted his story on the Internet "because it shows that you don't have to be a certain age to start to appreciate [Buddhism]. Questioning and seeking a higher purpose is part of human life that is felt especially strongly by young people."[11]

Afterlife

Afterlife—living in another world after the physical body dies—has been a common belief since ancient times. Ancient Egyptians, for example, commonly buried their dead with personal items that would help their souls throughout eternity. Royalty were buried in tombs with planting and cooking tools, items such as amulets to bring good fortune, and perhaps a boat for travel in the hereafter.

Ancient Greeks believed the dead went to an underworld ruled by a god known as Hades or Pluto, who judged whether the deceased were good or evil. Evildoers might be punished and sent to a lower place, but most Greeks expected their souls to go on to paradise. Reincarnation was also a possibility, with Hades deciding where the souls would be reborn.

Like the Greeks, ancient Hebrews (the Jewish people) believed in an underworld called She'ol where both the wicked and the righteous souls resided. But the Hebrews did not focus on the afterlife. Instead they believed that the devout received their rewards and the unjust got their punishment while they were on earth.

Currently, a majority of Americans believe in an afterlife. In fact, the Pew Research Center reported that "roughly seven-in-ten (72%) Americans say they believe in heaven" and "at the same time, 58% of U.S. adults also believe in hell."[12]

In 2016, NBC News reported on another study by a team at San Diego State University, Florida Atlantic University, and Case Western Reserve University. NBC's Maggie Fox reported that the team found "fewer Americans prayed, believed in God . . . or had confidence in religious institutions." Psychologist Jean Twenge of San Diego State led the study and noted, "The large declines in religious practice among young adults are also further evidence that millennials are the least religious generation in memory, and possibly in American history." Nevertheless, 80 percent of participants in the study still believed in an afterlife.[13]

Although most religious groups share the basic belief that the soul departs the body and after judgment may be destined for an eternal life in a heaven or a hell, there are numerous variations on the way religious groups perceive an afterlife. According to Orthodox Jewish beliefs, the dead will be resurrected when the Messiah appears and there will be eternal life after death. Righteous souls, meanwhile, can enjoy a place similar to the Garden of Eden and the wicked suffer in fiery pits.[14]

Some conservative Jews believe that upon the coming of the Messiah, there will be physical life after death, while others contend that there is a spiritual afterlife in which the living sense and remember the deceased. "Texts from every era in Jewish life identify a world where people go when they die," according to Rabbi Evan Moffic. "In the Bible it's an underworld called Sheol. In the rabbinic tradition it's known by a number of names, including the yeshiva shel mallah, the school on high. The Hebrew word for skies, shamayim, also came to refer to heaven."[15]

Many Christian denominations believe in the Second Coming of Christ, which will be accompanied by the resurrection of the righteous (or believers in Jesus

Christ). Faith in Jesus Christ and renouncing one's sins are essential if the resurrected soul is to achieve eternal life in heaven. Hell is reserved for those who do not accept Christ as their savior.[16]

Unlike Protestant denominations, the Roman Catholic Church believes there is a temporary place between heaven and hell called purgatory. Here souls may be tormented and purged of their sins and then ascend to heaven. The Greek Orthodox Church believes that the soul separates from the physical body immediately upon death, and that a partial judgment begins regarding the character of the person during his or her lifetime. This is considered a foretaste of heaven and hell.

The Religious Society of Friends (known as Quakers) is a faith that is like Christianity but it has no religious dogma, and members have diverse attitudes about the possibility of an afterlife. Nearly all Friends believe that speculations about the afterlife are not as important as attempts to improve the conditions of humanity in the present time. Some Friends trust that whatever good or evil works people do in this life may go on in the lives of those of the next generations. Another view is that the human spirit survives and is a continuation of this life—perhaps moving ahead to more advanced states through reincarnation. Still other Friends contend that the souls of the dead go to either heaven or hell, determined by how one lives while on earth.[17]

A world religion known as Baha'i, or a follower of Baha'u'llah, is often thought to be an offshoot of Islam but is instead an independent faith founded in Persia. Followers of Baha'u'llah believe that the essence of humans is the soul, but that they cannot fully understand what happens to the soul after death. Yet earthly existence is thought to be preparation for an afterlife, or a spiritual journey that has no ending.

Baha'i believers do not, however, accept the concept of reincarnation or transmigration of the soul. Neither do they believe in a physical heaven or hell. Instead, the Baha'i faith recognizes that the afterlife is a time of spiritual development for the righteous and perhaps a time of remoteness from God for unbelievers.[18]

Only a limited number of Unitarian Universalists (UUs) believe in an afterlife. And very few believe in a heaven or hell. If there is some kind of immortality, UUs believe it is revealed in the legacy they leave after their death. However, UUs have no shared dogma or absolute religious views. Members of the UU church are free to make their own decisions about life and death. The UU organization puts it this way:

Unitarian Universalist views about life after death are informed by both science and spiritual traditions. Many of us live with the assumption that life does not continue after death, and many of us hold it as an open question, wondering if our minds will have any awareness when we are no longer living. Few of us believe in divine judgment after death. It's in our religious DNA: the Universalist side of our tradition broke with mainstream Christianity by rejecting the idea of eternal damnation.[19]

Native American spirituality and their beliefs in an afterlife are seldom understood by most Americans or organized religions. In fact, as Arlene Hirschfelder and Paulette Molin write in the *Encyclopedia of Native American Religions: An Introduction,*

> Many Indian religious practitioners resent discussions about the specifics of their spiritual traditions, which they consider private, sacred, and powerful legacies of their people. They feel certain concepts and vocabulary are not always communicable. They are deeply concerned that sacred information that becomes public will lose its power or that it will be misused, which can be detrimental not only to Indian people but to all people.[20]

In general, however, numerous indigenous tribes hold feasts for the dead in the belief that spirits of the deceased return to take part in gifts of food and other items. Most feasts for the dead also include tribal dances. The Shawnee hold an annual feast "to honor the spirits of the deceased that is conducted mainly in the home rather than as a public observance. . . . Food is prepared and served on a table in a room, and a person, selected for the role, speaks to the spirits." After the family leaves the room, "food remains on the table for a number of hours. It is believed that the spirits participate in the feast but they eat only the spiritual part of the food."[21]

Apocalypse

The word *apocalypse* often suggests death—massive death—and the end of the world. The meaning of apocalypse may stem from the Persian prophet Zoroaster, who lived about 1500 BCE and believed that a battle between good and evil would destroy the universe but end in a perfect world. Today, the term means any revelation or disclosure, but when capitalized, it refers to the specific revelations of the future given to St. John as told in Revelation, the final book in the biblical New Testament. St John's revelation is in the style of the prophets of the Old Testament, couched in metaphors and horrifying images that are open to interpretation by believers.

The most famous of the revelations is the coming of the end times, when a great beast, known in Christian prophesies as the antichrist, will appear upon the earth. According to Revelation, the beast will be identified by a wound upon his head that has healed or the number 666. The antichrist will deceive humankind, and with the help of a false prophet (a religious leader) will establish a political and religious system that controls the entire world, leading to the destruction of Earth and all but the righteous.

Throughout recorded history, many predictions have been made about the end of the world based on major planetary alignments, wars, efforts for world peace, and numerous other events. In addition, prominent persons have been called the antichrist because of particular characteristics. The latter part of the book of Revelation describes nearly every kind of imaginable catastrophe that can befall a "sinful" world: famine, war, plagues, and natural disasters such as earthquakes. Essentially, the world feels the terrible wrath of God until the Second Coming of Jesus Christ, who will, according to the prophecy, establish God's kingdom where the righteous will prevail.

To this day, the story of the Apocalypse is told in contemporary versions— movies, videos, novels, comic books, and other media. Some believe the Apocalypse is a literal road map for events that will happen in the end times. Others see the story as literature full of symbolism, fantastic beasts, and a host of dramatic images.

Cryonics

Cryonics is a view about afterlife (or perhaps "reintroduced" life) that involves freezing the body of a person who has just died. According to cryonics theory, freezing preserves the body indefinitely for possible future re-suscitation when there is a cure for the disease that caused death. The Cryonics Institute located in Clinton Township, Michigan, states on its website,

Cryonics involves cooling a recently deceased person to liquid nitrogen temperatures in order to keep the body preserved indefinitely. Our goal is to keep the patient preserved until future science is able to repair or replace vital tissues and ultimately revive the patient. It might seem like an impossible goal to "revive" a "dead" person. However, "dying" is a process rather than an event. A majority of the body's tissues remain intact at a cellular level even after the heart stops beating. The goal of cryonics is to halt that process as quickly as possible after legal death, giving future physicians the best possible chance of reviving the patient. . . . We believe that this will happen in a future where our lifespans can be significantly, even radically, extended.[c]

One cryopreserved patient was baseball great Ted Williams. But his preservation was controversial. Williams's daughter sued her stepbrother and stepsister who had their father's body placed in a cryonics facility. The daughter who brought the suit argued that her father's will stipulated that he wanted to be cremated.

In November 2016, the body of a fourteen-year-old British girl was cryonically preserved. Known only as JS (because she was a minor), the teenager had a rare form of cancer and before her death had been asked to explain why she requested cryonics. She said, "I'm only 14 years old and I don't want to die, but I know I am going to. I think being cryopreserved gives me a chance to be cured and woken up, even in hundreds of years' time. I don't want to be buried underground. I want to live and live longer and I think that in the future they might find a cure for my cancer and wake me up. I want to have this chance. This is my wish."[d]

The teenager's mother agreed with her daughter's decision and made the arrangements. Her body was packed in dry ice and sent to the United States, where it was preserved at the Cryonics Institute at a reported cost of about $46,000. The facility said the teenager was its 143rd patient. An institute spokesperson told CNN, "A person held in such a state is said to be a 'cryopreserved patient,' because we do not regard the cryopreserved person as being inevitably 'dead.'"[e]

Special Days for the Dead

A Roman Catholic religious observance All Souls Day is celebrated on November 2 unless this date is a Sunday; then the observance is on November 3. All Souls Day commemorates the faithful who have died and are believed to be in purgatory. According to Roman Catholic teaching, purgatory is a place or condition of temporal punishment for the deceased who are not entirely free from faults or sins. It is believed that the Catholic faithful can help those in purgatory with prayers and by doing charitable deeds and attending mass.

In North America and Europe, Catholics traditionally visit family graves and may have a graveside meal on All Souls' Day. This is particularly true in Mexico and in Mexican American communities in the southwestern United States where the Day of the Dead is celebrated on November 1 and November 2.

All Souls Day and *Día de los Muertos* (Day of the Dead) are similar celebrations that remember the deceased. In Mexico and in Mexican American communities in the United States, events combine the rituals of the Roman Catholic All Souls Day with Mexican Indian traditions. *Día de los Muertos* is a two-day celebration that begins on the evening of October 31 and ends on November 2.

The Day of the Dead celebration originated an estimated three thousand years ago and was held in the summer during the Aztec month of Miccailhuitontli, named for the goddess Mictecacihuatl (Lady of the Dead). But Roman Catholic priests who came to what is now Mexico with Spanish conquerors in the 1500s tried to change the holiday from what they considered an irreverent celebration to a religious observance. So they proclaimed that the Day of the Dead would coincide with All Hallows Eve.

However, Days of the Dead are not like the U.S. Halloween observance with its many frightening and spooky images of ghosts and the dead rising from graves. A "major difference between the two holidays is who is involved," wrote Courtney Rae, of Jenison, Michigan, for *Teen Ink*. "Halloween, for the most part, is for children—who dress up, collect candy, and have parties—with adults supervising and handing out treats. El Día de los Muertos, on the other hand, is a family holiday for the living and the dead."[22]

The Mexican and Mexican American holiday honors and remembers deceased loved ones and is an acceptance of death; it recognizes that the cycle of life and death is inevitable. November 1 is the day when deceased angelitos (little angels) or infants and young children are honored. Deceased adults are remembered on November 2.

In Mexico and the United States, especially in the Southwest, many families visit cemeteries on November 2 to hold candlelight vigils and make offerings. The annual Los Angeles festival for the dead, for example, is held at the Hollywood Forever Cemetery, and several thousand people gather to celebrate both life and death, the continuity of the life cycle. Traditional music, foods, skeleton costumes and masks, candles, and cenpazuchilt flowers (yellow-orange marigolds) are part of the celebration. Usually the flowers are arranged in bouquets but the petals may also be strewn on the ground to guide the spirits of the dead.

For many who participate, the Days of the Dead reinforce the belief that death is merely a passage to eternal life. Celebrations require days of preparation.

In Mexico, it is common for a mariachi band wearing skeleton masks to perform at a Day of the Dead celebration. In the United States, mariachi musicians also play during Day of the Dead festivities. © *iStock.com/cadenamartin*

Family members may create or purchase *papel picado* (cut-paper art), decorate wreaths and crosses, and make traditional foods.

Preparations vary by region, but include baking *pan de los muertos* (bread of the dead), which may be candied fruit bread or egg bread shaped into the form of a person or baked in loaves with ceramic heads stuck into the surfaces. Breads may be embellished with braided dough, painted with food coloring, or sprinkled with colored sugar to achieve a festive effect. Candies made from a sugar paste and shaped like animals or skulls are traditional as is flan, a caramelized egg custard. A main dish is pork-and-chicken tamales wrapped in banana leaves rather than the usual corn husks, roasted pork loin, and chili sauces. Many families prepare home altars to commemorate deceased members. Common items on the altar table include the dead person's photograph, favorite foods, flowers, candles, incense, hot chocolate, *pan de los muertos*, and sweets.

Day of the Dead celebrations in Minnesota have taken place annually at the Minneapolis Institute of Art (MIA). The events have included *ofrendas*, individual alters or offerings made by teenagers to honor a dead loved one; if no one close has died, the *ofrenda* honors the day itself. Like home altars, the teen *ofrendas* are a collection of items representing a loved one and placed inside a box or wooden crate. In one early MIA celebration in 2009, "All of the *ofrendas* were created in crates, used to symbolize the migrant workers who came to the United States looking to support their families," Marianne Combs wrote in a post for the *State of the Arts* blog. "18-year old Tameka Boyce chose to use her ofrenda to honor her grandmother, who died in 2004 The crate [was] filled with pink, her grandmother's favorite color, a poem she wrote and candles with the names of different family members." Boyce was excited about her *ofrenda*, telling Combs, "It's great! It's surprising that my artwork's in the MIA. I can brag about it, it's very cool, my family's very interested and proud of me."[23]

Olga Guzmán also made an *ofrenda* for the MIA exhibit, but since she had not lost anyone close, she constructed a traditional *ofrenda*, "depicting skeletons dancing, singing and sharing a meal." Guzmán said at the time "I'm really busy—working, going to school, writing papers—and I don't get a chance to be creative with art. So I really love when a chance like this comes along because I feel my creative side can come out."[24] Video of some *ofrendas* and the teens who have created them appear on https://www.pinterest.com/pin/20266267046630870/.

Other student-made *ofrendas* have been displayed at various art museums and galleries around the nation, such as the Mexic-Arte Museum in Austin, Texas; the Memphis Brooks Museum of Art in Memphis, Tennessee; and the Oakland Museum of California.

LEGAL MATTERS

"Having a lot more money than the people you're close to seems to mean you have two choices, neither of which is great. . . . You can be secretive about your wealth or you can share it with them, but then you're in this weird position of economic power. I felt there was a third choice: you could just change the situation and decide not to have lots more money than people you're close with."—Greg, after receiving a large inheritance[1]

Whatever the religious and secular beliefs about death, there are also legal issues related to death that you should consider. Some legal matters may not have a direct effect on you at the time you read this, but it is important to have information available should you or people close to you need it. For example, if you are hospitalized for a serious injury or illness, you should know your rights regarding medical treatment. As described previously, the right to make such a decision is limited for minors unless a state has a mature minor doctrine.

Mature Minor Doctrine

The mature minor doctrine is a common-law rule that allows some preteens and teenagers to give consent to medical procedures if they can show that they are mature enough to make a decision on their own. If the minor is considered capable, parental consent may not be needed. Most states, however, do not recognize this doctrine. When the mature minor rule is applied, the medical procedures are usually not serious.

"One especially vexing problem in these circumstances is establishing if and when adolescents acquire the legal capacity to consent or not to diagnostics and treatment in general medical settings; this problem is particularly knotty where the law appears to be inconsistent with established ethical norms," wrote Doriane Lambelet Coleman and Philip M. Rosoff in the medical journal *Pediatrics.* "It arises when parents or guardians are unavailable at the time medical decisions are being considered, when adolescents disagree with their parents or their doctors about the course of their treatment, or more simply when adolescents express an independent view about that treatment." The authors explained,

It is well understood in the medical community that adolescents' aptitude to make rational, responsible decisions changes over time and that older teenagers and young adults have substantially similar cognitive capacities. These neurobiological facts, together with an increasingly prevalent ethical sense that especially older adolescents deserve to be treated as autonomous medical decision-makers, have caused some medical professionals to believe that children after ages 12 or 13 who appear to be mature have or ought to have the right to consent or to withhold consent to general medical treatment. This ethically derived right is often described in the medical literature as the "mature minor rule" or the "mature minor doctrine."[2]

A case in point is that of fourteen-year-old Dennis Lindberg of Mount Vernon, Washington, who was legally considered mature enough to decide his treatment for acute lymphocytic leukemia, a cancer of the bone marrow. (Washington was the first state to establish the mature minor doctrine.) In 2007, Dennis was confined to Seattle's Children's Hospital and Regional Medical Center. "Doctors said he needed blood transfusions to survive potentially lifesaving cancer treatments. But as a practicing Jehovah's Witness, Lindberg refused. . . . Jehovah's Witnesses believe accepting a blood transfusion violates God's law," according to Seattlepi.com. Dennis had the support of an aunt—also a Jehovah's Witness and legal guardian—with whom he had been living for four years. Dennis's parents were recovering from illicit drug use at a rehabilitation facility, but they publicly objected to Dennis's refusal to accept a blood transfusion. "My feelings have run the gamut from anger to tears not knowing who to believe and not to believe," Dennis Lindberg Sr. told reporter Cherie Black. "My sister has done a good job of raising him for the past four years, but her religious beliefs shouldn't be imposed on my son." Young Dennis died on November 27, 2007.[3]

A similar case occurred in Texas in 2015, when fifteen-year-old Noah Stacy with rare bone cancer refused chemotherapy. With his parents' and the state's approval he opted for alternative treatments that included what Noah called a "green diet." He told a Fox News reporter, "I want to take the natural approach. . . . Eat just green vegetables. Everything green." The diet was not all green vegetables, however. Noah's "natural" diet also included fresh oranges, strawberries, bananas, lemons, red peppers, lemons, and beets. Although doctors disapproved of the regimen, Noah insisted he felt better and his mother told Fox News, "Even if he doesn't make it through this, I'd rather him have a nice next six months of

It Happened to Cassandra

Cassandra Callender of Connecticut was not able to make her own decision about her health care. Her state did not have a mature minor doctrine. Seventeen-year-old Cassandra was diagnosed with Hodgkin's lymphoma in September 2014. At first she agreed to chemotherapy treatments, but both she and her mother wanted to try holistic remedies. Cassandra refused to go to the hospital for chemotherapy and ran away from home in protest. When she returned, "the state Department of Children and Families stepped in and a Juvenile Court judge removed her from her home, placed her under guard in the Connecticut Children's Medical Center and ordered her to undergo chemo," according to an AP report. "Her case went to the state Supreme Court, which ruled in January 2015 that Connecticut's Department of Children and Families wasn't violating her rights."[a]

When her cancer went into remission, Cassandra was allowed to return home. But in April 2016, a malignant mass was found in Cassandra's lungs. Shortly thereafter, when she turned eighteen, she was able to follow through on her decision to try natural alternative cancer treatments in Mexico. As of June 2017, her cancer had returned and she decided to undergo chemotherapy.

being happy and energetic, instead of being dragged down by chemotherapy." On July 28, 2016, sixteen-year-old Noah died.[4]

The Patient Self-Determination Act

The Patient Self-Determination Act (PSDA), passed by the U.S. Congress in 1990, is a federal law that requires most health-care providers to inform patients—including adolescents and young adults—about advance directives such as a living will and durable power of attorney (or medical power of attorney) for health-care decisions. The PSDA was designed to let patients know they have a right to communicate their wishes about the extent of medical treatment should death be imminent and they are incapacitated or in a permanent vegetative state. Patients who sign an advance directive form provide instructions on what kind of medical care they want if they are unconscious or too ill to communicate. This includes accepting or refusing medical or surgical treatment.

If you are eighteen years old or older, you can complete a legal will. © iStock.com/BrianA Jackson

When patients enter a hospital, hospice, or other health-care facility, they should receive a brochure or pamphlet explaining the PSDA. The publication also should explain patients' rights under state laws governing advance directives and the right to make decisions concerning medical care, including the right to accept or refuse medical or surgical treatment. Although health-care providers are permitted to contract with other entities to furnish this information, they are still legally responsible for ensuring that the requirements of this section are met. Other provisions of the law include the requirement that institutions educate their staff concerning its policies and procedures on advance directives and provide community education about them.

A final provision of the PSDA focuses on individuals who at the time of admission to a health-care facility are incapacitated—perhaps, for example, because of a vehicle accident or serious illness. In such cases, the health-care provider may give advance directive information to the individual's family or surrogate in accordance with state law. Each state has developed such a summary for hospitals, nursing homes, and home health agencies to use.

Wills and Bequests

Usually people think of a will as a document that elderly adults create. However, anyone eighteen years of age or older may complete a legal will, a document that specifically states how a person's estate (money, real estate, personal belongings, and so forth) should be distributed after her or his death. A will can be completed with a lawyer's assistance, by downloading a form from the Internet and completing it, or simply writing a document, signing it, and dating it. The latter is called a holographic will, and less "than half of all states recognize this type of will. It is very vulnerable to challenges in probate court," according to Attorneys.com.[5]

"Probate court is a specialized type of court that deals with the property and debts of a person who has died," wrote Edward A. Haman, on LegalZoom.com. "The basic role of the probate court judge is to assure that the deceased person's creditors are paid, and that any remaining assets are distributed to the proper beneficiaries."[6]

It Happened to the Laboz Sisters

In 2015, the Laboz sisters—Marlena, who was twenty-one at the time, and Victoria, who was seventeen—learned that they would inherit $10 million each as specified in their father Maurice Laboz's will. But their multimillionaire father had stipulated certain conditions regarding his daughters' inheritance. These requisites were reported by the *New York Post*:

- Marlena will get $500,000 for tying the knot, but only if her husband signs a sworn statement promising to keep his hands off the cash.

- She nets another $750,000 if she graduates "from an accredited university" and writes "100 words or less describing what she intends to do with the funds"—with the trustees appointed by her dad to oversee her money responsible for approving her essay.

- Both daughters get a big incentive to earn decent salaries by 2020. Each young woman is guaranteed to receive an annual payout of three times the income listed on their personal federal tax return. . . .

- If the daughters have kids and don't work outside the house, the trustees will give them each 3 percent of the value of their trust every Jan. 1. . . . The money flows only for a "child born in wedlock."

- The sisters could earn the same amount being "a caregiver" to their mother, Ewa Laboz, 58, whom their father was in the middle of divorcing. She got nothing in the will [due to a prenuptial agreement] and has indicated that she will contest it.[b]

Young people often receive gifts that are specified in their parents' or grand-parents' wills. In some wills, the gifts are called bequests. Bequests may also be separate documents that name specific individuals to receive, say, a diamond ring, stamp collection, motorcycle, car, paintings, or other property.

Often bequests are made to organizations such as Special Olympics, Partner-ship for Drug-Free Kids, Doctors without Borders, Planned Parenthood, Ameri-can Red Cross, Teen Cancer America, Humane Society of the United States, and countless other charitable groups.

Bequests and Wills of the Past

Bequests are often called endowments, and in past centuries endow-ments were published and the documents posted in public places. These documents were rather like contracts to make certain that the dead person's will was actually carried out and not simply forgotten. It was also customary for a religious leader to read these documents to parishioners or print them in the church registry along with records of births and deaths.

During the fifteenth to the eighteenth centuries, people would specify in their wills the place they wanted to be buried, preferably in a vault within a church or cathedral, rather than on the grounds. In some instances, the will actually con-tained specific measurements to indicate where the person wanted their remains placed: near a certain statue or close to the altar.

Early wills sometimes designated a specific person to make a religious pil-grimage on behalf of the deceased. The designated person would make the pilgrimage for a specified fee, to be paid on return. The practice of making a pilgrimage for a deceased person has carried over to the present time and also has been dramatized in films.

Before tombstones and monuments became an important part of the funeral process, endowment tablets were of great significance. They were made of copper, brass, or marble, and engraved with the name of the deceased and the day and year of death. Often nearby but eventually on the tablets themselves would be an art rendition of the deceased person in some attitude of prayer or meditation.

When bequests go to schools, hospitals, human rights groups, religious organizations, and other national, state, and local institutions, you could easily be a beneficiary. For example, you might benefit if someone makes a bequest of computers that you use in a school program or funds for a sports, band, or art program to which you belong. Perhaps a bequest provides funds for a local ball park or swimming pool or skateboard ramp. Such a bequest benefits anyone who makes use of these facilities.

Organ Donations

Tens of thousands of people in the United States await organ transplants—hearts, livers, kidneys—as well as eyes and tissues. You can arrange such a donation by completing a Uniform Donor Card or the organ donation form on the back of your driver's license. Those who plan to donate their organs for transplants usually carry the donor card with instructions about disposal of their remains if deceased.

Cody Souders, an eighteen-year-old college freshman of Easton, Pennsylvania, had told his parents that he wished to be an organ donor. But he had no idea that his wish would soon be granted. In 2013, Cody accidentally took an overdose of prescription drugs. He was hospitalized on life support for five days but did not survive. His parents immediately granted his wishes and donated his organs. "His donations benefitted more than 50 people in all," according to CBS News. "His heart, liver, and both kidneys provided life-saving transplants. His corneas restored sight, his skin helped burn victims, and dozens of other tissues and body parts including bones, tendons, valves and veins assisted patients in need." CBS reported that Cody's brother Justin said, "'I like the idea that he's still living on today in other people' and his younger sister commented 'People take everything for granted, they have no idea how precious every moment is.'"[7]

Another organ donor was South Carolina fifteen-year-old Jasmine Lampkin. She died in an ATV accident on Labor Day Weekend in 2016. She was not wearing a helmet and "suffered severe head trauma from the fall," according to WCBD/WNCN. She died from her injuries and her father donated her organs; her "heart went to a 15-year-old Pennsylvania girl—saving her life."[8]

A Utah teenager, London Layton, died unexpectedly on December 11, 2015. London was fifteen and died of complications from diabetes. "In a twist of fate, the day before she died, London and her mom were at the DMV [Department of Motor Vehicles]," apparently so London could apply for her driver's license. London's mother Torrie explained that the application asks "Do you want to be a donor?" After learning what that meant, London marked "yes" on the form.

London's parents donated her body and their "daughter's heart valve, her corneas and her leg bones saved other lives and they also donated her hair to Locks of Love," according to a news report.[9]

Recipients of Organ Donations

The National Organ Transplant Act of 1984 established a task force to examine medical, ethical, legal, economic, and social issues related to organ transplantation and prohibited the buying and selling of organs. Many deceased whose organs are donated are victims of car accidents or gunshot wounds that cause fatal injuries. In some cases, patients are brain dead—their brain functions have ceased permanently, but their heart and lungs continue to function with the use of ventilators. Families may make the difficult decision to discontinue the use of life-sustaining equipment and allow surgery to remove organs for transplantation.

Those who receive donations include young people like Carlee of Texas. Carlee has received two heart transplants—one when she was just one and a half years old, the second when she was thirteen. Her first transplant occurred because her heart was enlarged and she was struggling to breathe. After the transplant, she had an active childhood, studying dance, and playing basketball and tennis. But at age thirteen her heart failed again and she had to be put on a waiting list for another transplant. Fortunately, a donated heart was found, and she was quickly rushed to the hospital for surgery. Although her recovery was slow, she rebuilt her strength and resumed an active life. "I feel like people who haven't experienced something like that . . . it's hard for them to realize how important life is," she said. Her story was posted when she was fifteen and she and friends her age were looking forward to getting their drivers licenses. Carlee planned to register as an organ donor and urged her friends to do so as well. "Those people who gave me another heart . . . they gave me a second chance. I've been saved twice by an organ donor. So who says I can't save somebody else," she declared.[10]

Another donor recipient whose story appears on OrganDonor.gov, was Patrick of Michigan. In his words,

At the age of five my vision began to deteriorate due to a scar on my left cornea. Suddenly I was no longer able to play outside with my friends. No longer able to read or play with Legos, no longer able to see the concerned faces of my family and friends. A slow shift occurred, from a five-year-old's bright mysterious world of endless possibilities, to a world of blurred shapes and colors. I was headed towards partial blindness, a condition that was averted by a decision, made by a couple that had just lost their son in an auto accident. Their decision to donate led to my corneal transplant, at the age of six, and changed my life. . . .

I feel, as I'm sure many recipients do, a drive and responsibility to use this phenomenal gift to its fullest; to use it not only to benefit my own life, but the lives of others. . . .

I wish I were eloquent enough to express the gratitude I feel to my donor family. I still wouldn't know what words to use to describe the awe, respect, and appreciation for the decision they made. A decision that was courageous and selfless and made at an incredibly difficult time. I say thank you and try to use my sight and my life to touch the lives of others.[11]

Whole Bodies for Science

When people designate that at the time of death they wish to donate their entire bodies to science, most medical schools pay for transportation of the deceased, limited by a specified distance (one hundred to several hundred miles) from a hospital or funeral home to the medical school. Some medical facilities may require the family or the estate of the deceased to pay transportation costs. After the donated body has served its purpose for scientific research, the medical institution may pay for cremation of the body and will return the cremated remains to family members upon their request. The ashes of the deceased may be returned to the family if written instructions are provided soon after death.

If there is no medical university in a state, the National Anatomical Service in Staten Island, New York, can locate the nearest institution or one that has the most need for cadavers. A body could be rejected if it has been burned extensively or badly injured. A body donation may be refused if the deceased has had surgery, is extremely obese or emaciated, or is in the beginning stages of decomposition. Alzheimer's disease, and the presence, or suspected presence, of contagious diseases such as hepatitis, AIDS, and tuberculosis are other criteria for refusing a body donation.

Some bodies donated to science are used immediately for research, while others may be held longer—up to three years—for study. When studies are complete, medical facilities cremate bodies.

Body donations have helped medical researchers develop drugs and therapies to treat many diseases and illnesses, including Alzheimer's, arthritis, heart disease, Parkinson's, and neurological disorders. A donated body also helps medical instructors teach human anatomy, new surgical procedures, and other medical techniques—education that is closer to reality than learning from textbooks or artificial cadavers.

Grave Robbers

If you watch horror movies or ghostly TV shows, you probably have seen actors portray fictitious grave robbers. However, grave robbers truly exist, and robbing graves is an ancient practice that still occurs in countries around the world. Even though it is a crime in most places today to desecrate burial sites, seldom are grave robbers caught, and if they are, they usually receive only light sentences or no convictions.

Archeologists have found evidence of grave robbing dating back to ancient times. Above-ground tombs of Egyptian Pharaohs, for example, have been plundered for gold, copper, precious stones, and other valuable artifacts buried with them. Even the graves of common folks were ransacked for whatever riches were there.

Ancient burial grounds in what is now Peru have also been sites popular with grave robbers. From the time of the Spanish conquest of the Incas in the 1500s to the present, gravesites have been looted. Plunderers have probed for treasures along the coast in the desert sands of northern Peru. The valuables found include gold, textiles, and pottery, some of it dating back more than two thousand years. Artifacts are then sold to middle men, who in turn sell to international buyers. During the 1990s, two Florida men were arrested for trying to sell a gold relic stolen from a Peruvian tomb. The price tag was $1.6 million.

In the United States, indigenous burial grounds across the nation have long been targets for looters, and desecration of graves has been increasing in spite of federal laws designed to protect them. Since the early 1980s, for example, more than eight hundred graves in Caddo Nation cemeteries in northeastern Texas have been looted, even though responsibility for overseeing these sites falls under the National Historic Preservation Act, the Archaeological Resources Protection Act, and the Native American Graves Protection and Repatriation Act. Looters and artifact buyers seldom if ever express any dismay over their illegal activities and violation of sacred lands.

In other states, particularly in the South and Southeast, indigenous cemeteries have frequently been robbed. For example, two people were photographed in January 2002 at Pine Island, Lee County, Florida, robbing indigenous graves in violation of state and federal laws, but the robbers were not caught.

Not all grave robbers over the centuries have sought valuable artifacts. From the sixteenth century until the early 1900s, graves were robbed to provide bodies for the study of anatomy and dissection at medical schools. During the 1700s and 1800s, prospective surgeons needed to study human anatomy but seldom had enough cadavers for dissection. Schools that taught anatomy were owned by university professors, who ran them for a profit. Because of the large number of schools and students, there was a need for many cadavers. However, there were strict laws regarding the use of cadavers, creating a shortage that resulted in body snatching. Thieves stole bodies from cemeteries, took the specimens to the schools, and received their payment from students or others at the schools.

Burial and Cemetery Laws

Every state and some counties in the United States have laws regarding burials, burial grounds, and cemeteries, although these laws vary. Most state laws prohibit disturbance of graves and when property that contains human remains is sold, the deed must indicate the presence of human burial sites. A buyer is obligated to protect such sites, unless the seller transfers the remains to another burial ground. Anyone who desecrates a grave or burial site commits a misdemeanor in most states.

Nearly all states have some type of historic preservation law that protects unmarked human burials and human skeletal remains on state and private lands. These laws for the most part are designed to prevent disturbance, destruction, and desecration of indigenous burial sites and to prevent looting of artifacts from Native American burial mounds. The laws usually state that any person who willfully and knowingly disturbs, destroys, removes, vandalizes, or damages unmarked human burials is guilty of a felony; failure to report such disturbance is also a felony.

Unfortunately, graves in some cemeteries have been vandalized, sometimes by teenagers who are under the mistaken notion that they are taking part in a daring prank. Or they think damaging cemeteries is a fun thing to do. Apparently, that was the case when a teenager damaged a Flat Rock, Michigan, cemetery in May 2016. A thirteen-year-old boy knocked over headstones in the historical Flat Rock Cemetery where graves dated back to the early 1800s. Social media posts helped authorities positively identify the culprit, who police determined toppled the headstones with karate kicks.[12]

In October 2016, two boys age twelve and fourteen vandalized Colonial Cemetery in Independence, Louisiana. A witness called parish deputies and Independence police, who discovered that "over 50 grave sites were damaged and 32 were broken into. Deputies said personal items left at the grave sites were damaged and some were broken. Multiple American flags were also found removed, damaged or thrown on the ground," according to WWLTV.com. Deputies located the teenager "hiding on top of a mausoleum in the cemetery." The police found the twelve-year-old "riding a bike nearby." The boys were arrested and "charged with 50 counts of criminal damage to property, 50 counts of desecration of a grave, and 32 counts of simple burglary."[13]

Restoring and Preserving Cemeteries

Countering young culprits who damage burial sites are numerous youth who help restore vandalized or abandoned cemeteries. Young people sometimes participate in projects undertaken by a legal entity such as a county or township commission that takes charge of preserving a cemetery if it has been abandoned. Or teenagers may start their own restoration efforts.

An example is fourteen-year-old Luke Matheis of Jacksonville, Missouri. Luke needed a project "to get to Eagle Scout," as he put it. His father had told him that a veterans' cemetery west of Jacksonville needed cleaning. The cemetery included graves of slaves and "a member of the 60th Regiment of the United States Colored Infantry during the Civil War," according to a news report. In 2015, Luke along with his Boy Scout team and community members, worked on the project. "Our [Scout] troop jumps on anything when you ask them to help. . . . They're all kind of helping each other get to Eagle Scout," Luke told TV reporter Chris Gothner.[14] The troop, along with some community members, cut down weeds, raked leaves, picked up broken tree limbs, mended fences, and restored toppled tombstones. The cleanup was completed in the summer of 2016. Photos of the renovated cemetery and Luke with his Eagle Scout badge are on Facebook.[15]

Another youth cemetery restoration project took place in New York City. Young people who were learning to repair and restore centuries-old gravestones worked as interns (trainees or apprentices) at Woodlawn Cemetery in the summer of 2016. Many of the interns had never been to the cemetery. Eighteen-year-old

Restoring a graveyard often involves cleaning and repairing headstones. © *iStock.com/ djedzura*

Teddy Espinal had hardly spent time in any graveyard. But he told Slate reporter Ella Morton, "I look at the cemetery differently now. . . . Before this I used to be like, 'Oh, dead people.' But now I think about stones, and maintaining and cleaning and working on stuff. It's less scary."[16]

Intern Melanie Ayala, twenty-three, grew up in a Mexican family and celebrated Day of the Dead each year, so she had no fear of burial sites or the dead. Ayala explained to Morton,

> I always talk to the headstones. . . . I was cleaning this one, her name was Sophia. Sophia Stark. And I was like, "I got you, Sophia. I'm going to clean you right up." I pay attention to the names, and I pay attention to the dates. . . . I saw a few headstones that had my birthday. It just makes you be happy that you're above ground for another day.[17]

Morton noted in her article that Ayala and other interns learn "a wide range of practical restoration skills," and they also "reflect on the nature of remembrance. Some of the inscriptions on the stones have become obscured by years of built-up dirt and biological growth. To carefully scrub that away and reveal the name of someone who died long ago is to revive their memory and honor their life—regardless of who they were."[18]

WHEN PETS AND SERVICE ANIMALS DIE

....

"Lucy was the light of my life. I was lucky to know her from the time I adopted
her at eight weeks to her final day in her 15th year. On our final car ride together, I
bought her french fries and a couple of hot dogs."—Becky Trac3y on BuzzFeed.com[1]

When the topic of death is discussed, seldom does it center on deceased pets, or companion animals as they are often called. And seldom do deaths of service animals, such as military dogs and assistance dogs for the disabled, come to mind. However, the deaths of these animals can be devastating to their human caretakers. Military and service dogs are especially missed when they die because they are needed for safety and protection.

Pet Loss

People who do not have a pet may not understand that a pet is not just a dog, cat, or some other animal. Rather, pets are like children, daily companions and beloved. Those who have never had a pet often advise people who have lost an animal companion to just get another one. Replacing a beloved pet is not a simple solution, however. Many pet owners say when their companion animal dies, it's like a death in the family or loss of a good friend; there must be time to grieve and mourn.

Jasmin is one person who felt the pain of pet loss and shared her experience, along with a photograph of her dog, on BuzzFeed:

> We got my dog Ben all the way back when I was 4. When I was 18, my dad mentioned getting Ben put down because he was so old and sick. He'd been getting weaker for a while; we couldn't take him on walks anymore, and he would have accidents without any warning at all.

Dogs, cats, and other pets are precious companions for many people, and when companion animals die, their loss can greatly distress humans. © iStock.com/TracyHornbrook

We got him a nice steak the day before we took him to the vets. When we were waiting in the vets, he had another accident and I felt horrible thinking maybe he knew it was happening. I stayed in the room and talked to him and petted him until he wasn't with us anymore. I'll never forget him and to honour him, when we got another dog we got a yellow Labrador like him, and gave it a name beginning with B.[2]

Another person who posted on BuzzFeed had lost a bird, a pet budgie, that she had had for many years, and she cuddled it on her chest while it died. A dog owner stated that she might get another dog but could not really replace her beloved Chloe. The owners of various other pets—a squirrel, a rat, a guinea pig, and several cats and dogs—also shared their stories about their last days with their pets. One cat lover "cradled his head and held his paw while he breathed his last." Many pet lovers fed their animals favorite foods before they died.[3]

A teenager from Staten Island, New York, wrote an essay for *Teen Ink* about the death of her cat, her first pet and best friend:

I remember the day you left very clearly. And boy, it was not pretty. I remember collapsing in tears, screaming that they couldn't take you away from me. Sobbing my heart out, only to face the reality that there was nothing I could do. Time passed and I didn't get any better. I hid my pain behind a fake smile and shining eyes. Shining from tears. I wanted to die. I couldn't imagine life without you, and I wished for you to come back to me. I missed you terribly, and I couldn't get you off my mind.[4]

When Clarissa Fallis lost her dog in a 2013 accident, she described the tragic details on Petful.com. Fallis explained that while a college student she had adopted a dog named Lynal who was trained to be a service dog (or an emotional support dog). She wrote, "Throughout my life I have battled depression, anxiety and panic attacks. I was able to keep it under control with typical medication and therapy until I was 18. My psychological state got harder to manage when a very close friend tragically passed away."[5]

Fallis noted that Lynal "not only helps me in public but gives me focus when I am having a difficult day with my disability." But one day on a walk with Fallis, the dog was not attached to his service vest and ran into a street where he was accidentally hit by a truck. He was instantly killed. "Losing my dog shattered my life, and I am still learning how to cope with my loss," Fallis wrote. "Every day presents itself with new challenges in a world in which my service dog no longer exists. I know I will have dozens of dogs in my lifetime, but Lynal will always be my first dog and the dog who taught me so much about myself."[6]

Help for Pet Loss

Some people seek advice and help for pet loss by accessing Internet sites such as the Association for Pet Loss and Bereavement (APLB) in Nutley, New Jersey. APLB recommends reading the award-winning book *The Loss of a Pet*, fourth edition, by Wallace Sife, PhD (2015). The book "is strongly endorsed by this association for use by individuals in deep mourning for their beloved pets," APLB states.[7]

On the website Pet Loss Support Page, Moira Anderson Allen has these words of advice for those who have suffered pet loss:

> During the years you spent with your pet (even if they were few), it became a significant and constant part of your life. It was a source of comfort and companionship, of unconditional love and acceptance, of fun and joy. So don't be surprised if you feel devastated by the loss of such a relationship. People who don't understand the pet/owner bond may not understand your pain. All that matters, however, is how you feel. Don't let others dictate your feelings: They are valid, and may be extremely painful. But remember, you are not alone: Thousands of pet owners have gone through the same feelings.[8]

Did You Know?

Burying deceased companion animals in a pet cemetery is becoming an increasingly accepted practice in the United States. There are hundreds of U.S. pet cemeteries, with the oldest one—Hartsdale Pet Cemetery in New York—established in 1896. Pet burial sites can be found in most states. These cemeteries are usually part of other animal-related businesses, such as veterinary clinics and hospitals, boarding kennels, and pet grooming and training facilities.

Some pet burial sites have been developed in separate sections of human cemeteries. In most U.S. pet cemeteries, the services provided are similar to those offered for deceased humans. People may opt to bury or cremate their pets and select caskets, cremation urns, tombstones, or other memorials for their dead animal companions.

Veterinarians can also help ease pain if you lose a pet. A California woman (call her Marla) had a longtime feline companion. When her cat died, she took the animal to a veterinarian for cremation, a sorrowful task. But afterward, the veterinarian presented Marla with a beautiful memorial—a wooden container with her cat's ashes. A name plate was on top, plus a locket and photograph of her cat. Although she still missed and mourned her pet, Marla was comforted by the memorial and pleasant reminders of her furry friend.

When Pets Are Abandoned

"Around 4 million dogs are abandoned every year in the USA alone," according to Animal-Rights-Action.com.[9] Most abandoned dogs that end up in animal shelters are of mixed origin, but purebreds are also picked up as strays and taken to rescue centers.

Dogs become strays for a variety of reasons. Some owners may be forced to give up their animals because of housing restrictions. Or people may move because of a job change and are unable to take their pets with them. The costs of animal upkeep may be an issue, or a family member or college roommate may

Abandoned pets may have to search for food and live under bridges, in culverts, or on public streets unless picked up and saved by animal shelters. © *iStock.com/DmyTo*

It Happened to Lily

They found a wounded dog named Lily. They saved her life. *They* were sixteen-year-old Cole Bodelson and his friends of Santa Fe, New Mexico. The teens were off-roading in 2014 and encountered a black Labrador who was blind and dying. "We saw her paw which had been severed all the way around, she was laying on her paw like protecting it, and we were afraid if we picked her up she would have like some kind of horrible wound under there," Cole explained on LifewithDogs.tv. The dog had been shot four times. Two bullets were still in her body. Cole and his friends took the dog to the Santa Fe Animal Shelter, where veterinarians had to amputate the rest of her injured leg. Even though Lily was blind, she regained her health at the shelter and eventually was adopted by a family in Albuquerque.[a]

---

develop an allergy to dog fur. Sometimes, pet owners cannot handle the responsibility of feeding, training, and maintaining an animal's health, so they may leave the animal in a remote place to fend for itself. Or perhaps a dog just runs out the door and does not come back.

Pit bulls and Chihuahuas are the most common dogs that become strays, according to numerous animal shelters and animal welfare websites. John Metcalfe, writing for CityLab.com, which reports on urban issues for the *Atlantic*, found that between 2011 and 2013, Chihuahuas were the most common dog in Los Angeles animal shelters at 13,833, and the runner-up was pit bulls at 7,767.[10] Michael J. Fox, who writes for the *Washington Post*, noted that "annually, an estimated 7.6 million animals enter shelters in the United States. Some 2.7 million of them are destroyed. Some shelters limit their holding time because of the many animals arriving daily."[11] Shelters may also euthanize animals because they are seriously ill or injured, and mercy killing is the compassionate solution.

Beware Puppy and Kitten Mills

The American Society for the Prevention of Cruelty to Animals (ASPCA), the Humane Society, Paws, Companion Animal Protection Society, and other animal welfare organizations warn people who want to obtain a pet to beware of stores that sell puppies and kittens produced by unlicensed breeders. A report published in *Rolling Stone* in 2017 describes the miserable, filthy, and sometimes deadly conditions of dog factories, better known as puppy mills. Magazine reporter Paul Solotaroff went with twenty staff members from the Humane Society, the sheriff and his deputies of Cabarrus County, North Carolina, and "a contingent of veterinarians from a local animal hospital" to investigate a rather nondescript small brick house in a rural area. On arrival, this is what they found:

> A stench of complex poisons pushed out: cat piss and dog shit and mold and bleach commingled into a cloud of raw ammonia that singed the hair in our nostrils. . . . [They] tiptoed around the filth underfoot into a house caked in pet fur and waste. Damp laundry draped across every flat surface; the floor was a maze of cat crates and garbage. From somewhere in the house, we heard the howling of dogs, but they weren't in the bedrooms or the tumbledown john or the kitchen piled high with dishes.[12]

In the basement, the investigative crew were faced with howling animals, "dozens of puppies in dust-cloaked cages. . . . There were Yorkies and poodles and Maltese mixes, but their fur was so matted and excrement-mottled it was hard to tell which from which. Bred for profit, most of them would have been sold in pet stores or on websites by their third or fourth month of life."[13]

The lengthy *Rolling Stone* article continues in gruesome detail about the cruelty and degradation of this homegrown breeding place owned by Patricia Yates, "who was arrested and charged with animal cruelty." Yates claimed she loved the dogs, but that hardly seemed the case as the investigators found yet more unhealthy animals, including "two poodles, both of them desperately underfed. . . . [One] was blind in both eyes and had thumb-size infections where his molars used to be."[14]

The North Carolina case, sadly, is not the only puppy mill operation. The ASPCA noted, "The highest concentration of puppy mills is in the Midwest, specifically in Missouri, but there are also high concentrations in other areas, including Pennsylvania, Ohio and upstate New York."[15]

What if you are eager to get a new companion animal and would like to acquire a puppy? Animal welfare groups caution to beware not only of puppy mills but also the stores that claim to be selling animals from legally licensed breeders. That claim may be false or misleading. If you want to be certain about where an animal was bred, check out that place yourself.

ASPCA warns as well about trying to find a dog by browsing the Internet. You may be bombarded with elaborate websites offering the offspring of "champions" with a host of fancy terms and pictures of adorable pups. Don't

Anyone looking to buy a pet should investigate its origin and whether the animal was a stray and is healthy. © *iStock.com/LewisTsePuiLung*

be fooled: Internet puppy scammers attract potential buyers with cute photos and phony promises. Hundreds of complaints are filed every year from victims who were scammed when buying a dog online—the puppy you receive may not be the puppy you agreed to buy, or you may not receive a puppy at all. Internet scams range from fake "free to good home" ads where the buyer is asked to pay for shipping, only to never see that puppy they tried to help, to breeders posing as sanctuaries or rescues, but charging upwards of $1,000 in "adoption" fees.[16]

Loss of Military Working Dogs

Approximately 2,700 military working dogs are active in the U.S. Armed Forces, many of them in Afghanistan and Iraq. Military dogs are heroes, and unfortunately there have been rumors that these dogs have been left behind when service men and women return home—rumors that are untrue, according to Rebecca Frankel, senior editor at *Foreign Policy* and author of a paperback *War Dogs: Tales of Canine Heroism, History, and Love* (2016). In a column she titled WdotW (War Dogs of the Week) she wrote, "So let me be clear: the U.S. military does *not* treat its dogs like dispensable pieces of equipment. And the U.S. military does *not* leave its dogs behind. And anyone repeating these untruths is not only doing the dogs

Read and Watch!

A Dog's Purpose: A Novel for Humans by W. Bruce Cameron (2011) and his follow-up book *A Dog's Journey: Another Novel for Humans* (2013) are two works of fiction that humanize dogs. Both books are best sellers, and the first is the basis for the film *A Dog's Purpose*, released in January 2017. Both book and film are narrated by a dog named Bailey who has died and has been reincarnated in four other canine lives. One reincarnation is Toby, born in the wild but rescued along with his family by a woman who cares for strays. The woman's shelter does not meet regulations and is shut down; Toby is sent to another facility where he is euthanized. Toby is reborn as a golden retriever—the narrator Bailey. The next rebirth is Ellie, a female German shepherd, and the final reborn life is a black Lab called Buddy. Throughout these varied lives, Bailey questions and searches for the purpose of his life. He finds meaning through his loving behavior and teaching his human companions to laugh and love. This story reminds readers the lives of all creatures have a purpose.

Cameron's two books are so instructive that a teacher study guide has been created about setting goals for one's life and reflecting on what can be learned and achieved before life ends. The guide also includes information and quotes regarding the author's purpose for writing the books. You can access the guide at http://www.brucecameron.com/images/a_dogs_purpose_a_dogs_journey_study-guide.pdf.

---

a tremendous disservice, but is, I worry, negatively impacting the future of the MWD [Military War Dog] program." Frankel pointed out that the military does not treat dogs as "equipment." In fact, a handler is always with his dog and vice versa. If a service member is injured or killed, another person takes the dog back to its unit. She explained further,

> When a dog's time in the military has come to an end and the dog is ready to retire, here's how it works: The dog is first put under review. This is an involved but expedited process that includes input from veterinarians, behaviorists, and guidance of that dog's home station's kennel master—

the person familiar with that dog's entire career. When it's determined that the dog is in good health and is of suitable temperament for life as a house dog, the military reviews the candidates who want to adopt the dog—oftentimes there is a long list of the dog's former handlers who are ready and willing to take him home. ("Home" in this case being a private residence.)[17]

One story about Sergeant Joshua (Josh) Ashley and his dog Sirius tells how the bond between them remained even after Ashley was killed in Afghanistan. Ashley's "friend Sgt. Frederick Roethler took over handling Sirius. But when Roethler heard that Ashley's family was looking to adopt the military working dog, he was more than happy to pass the leash," wrote James Clark on TaskandPurpose. com. Roethler noted, "Sgt. Ashley and Sirius are one and the same person, and that family needs to be brought together with Sirius. . . . It's amazing to see it finally happening and his family is able to have a little bit more closure and they get to have something else in their lives that will get to remind them every day of everything that they loved about Josh."[18]

Another demonstration of a MWD's faithfulness was Labrador retriever Hawkeye, who stayed beside the coffin of Navy SEAL Jon Tumilson, who was killed in Afghanistan in 2011. Tumilson's funeral was in his hometown of Rockford, Iowa. Hawkeye attended the funeral, walked up to the casket before the service, and lay down beside it. He stayed there for the entire funeral. The media and Internet sites quickly publicized the dog's response to Tumilson's death.

How War Dogs Are Honored

When military dogs die in combat, they are memorialized in a variety of ways. For example, a U.S. Marine Corps German shepherd that lost a leg sniffing out a roadside bomb in Afghanistan was awarded the world's highest honor for service dogs during a special ceremony in London on April 5, 2016, according to Fox News, which reported that

> Lucca, who served U.S. troops during more than 400 missions in Iraq and Afghanistan over a six-year span, received the People's Dispensary for Sick Animals (PDSA) Dickin Medal at the Wellington Barracks in London. She is the first Marine Corps dog to receive the medal, considered the top honor for war animals around the world. Her handler, Gunnery Sgt. Christopher Willingham, told Sky News that it was an "incredible honor" to receive the award from the veterinary charity. "It is very humbling to be part of this entire process," he said. "I think more importantly is that

A Star Military Dog

Max is a 2015 film based on actual events about a military dog whose Marine trainer, Kyle Wincott, died in Afghanistan combat. One compelling scene in the film takes place at Wincott's funeral when Max and several Marines attend to pay their respects to their comrade. Max on a leash struggles and whimpers as he tries to get down the church aisle to the coffin. When Max pulls free, he places his front paws on the flag-draped coffin, then lies down beside it, obviously demonstrating that he is mourning.

The story then focuses on the Wincott family: the parents, Pamela and Ray, and Kyle's adolescent brother, Justin, who resents the heroic Marine. Justin also shows contempt for his father, who appears to have favored Kyle during his sons' childhood. The family eventually decides to adopt Kyle's war dog, even though they are warned that the dog may be unable to adapt to civilian life and could be dangerous.

As the story progresses, Justin, in spite of his disdain for all things adult, begins to relate to Max and Max to him. They achieve a close bond while another subplot develops. It involves a military friend of Kyle's, Tyler Harne, who is from the same small town in Texas. Tyler returns to their hometown and fuels Justin's resentment with false tales that Max attacked Kyle and caused Kyle's weapon to discharge and kill him. This is just one of many Tyler falsehoods that cover his shenanigans with a gang selling illegal weapons.

Weaving in and out of the story is Max, who comes close to being euthanized because of Tyler. But Justin and his bike-riding friends release Max and the dog engages with Justin's avid bike riding and racing. Max also protects Justin when he confronts problems. Will Max's fate be revealed in the end? What do you think?

Lucca's accomplishments are going to help bring awareness and recognition to all our military working dogs and their handlers."[19]

Deceased MWDs are honored with the United States War Dogs Memorial, located near the Vietnam Memorial in Holmdel, New Jersey. The bronze memorial for the MWDs is a statue of a Vietnam War soldier kneeling beside his dog. It was dedicated on June 10, 2006. Although the memorial represents war dog teams of the Vietnam War, it also honors all U.S. war dogs and their handlers—past, present, and future.

Do Animals Grieve like Humans?

In the story about Jon Tumilson and his dog Hawkeye, *U.S. News* reporter Mary-ann Mott wrote,

> Grief is one of the basic emotions dogs experience, just like people, said Dr. Sophia Yin, a San Francisco-based veterinarian and applied animal behaviorist. Dogs also feel fear, happiness, sadness, anger, as well as possessiveness. Dogs who mourn may show similar signs to when they're separated for long periods of time from the individual they're bonded to, she said. Of those signs, depression is the most common, in which dogs usually sleep more than normal, move slower, eat less, and don't play as much.
>
> The beginnings of such a strong inter-species bond between humans and dogs dates back some 15,000 years, when early man and the ancestor of today's dog roamed the Earth together.
>
> Today, after thousands of years of friendship, there's a great deal of attunement between humans and dogs, not only in terms of comprehension of each other's gestures and body language but also emotionally.[20]

Military dogs like Hawkeye are not the only animals known to mourn. Anecdotes from animal owners, caretakers, and researchers often describe how pets or other animals grieve. Skeptics suggest that stories about grieving animals are anthropomorphism—attributing human characteristics to animals, plants, or other natural phenomena. Although no hard science confirms animal mourning, Barbara King, a professor of anthropology at the College of William and Mary, details in her book *How Animals Grieve* (University of Chicago Press, 2013) numerous demonstrations of animals—cats, dogs, elephants, goats, and others—grieving. In an interview with NPR, King explained,

> In the book, I tell stories—some gleaned from the scientific literature, others from interviews with animal caretakers—of individual animals and how they expressed love for a relative or friend, then grieved when that other animal died. . . .
>
> I also describe field scientists who use GPS collars to track elephants' movements then closely observe the behavior of individuals as they approach the body of a dead matriarch . . . [and] changes experienced by

monkeys who have lost kin. . . . Video, too, is revolutionizing the study of animal emotion; when we film what happens as an animal is dying or dies, we can assess the behaviors by rewatching and coding the tapes, rather than by making snap judgments about what's unfolding quickly in real time.[21]

Not only do animals demonstrate grief when companions or caretakers die, they also sense when a human is near death. Numerous news articles, magazine features, and Internet sites have reported stories about cats and dogs that apparently can predict death or can sense that a companion is ill and comfort her or him. David Gutierrez, staff writer for NaturalNews.com notes,

Anyone who has lived with a dog can attest to the fact that dogs can sense when people are sad and will often seek to comfort them. However, evidence suggests that dogs might also be able to sense when people are ill or even dying and increase their comforting attention accordingly. Even when humans cannot tell that another person is suffering, dogs might be able to detect physical or emotional ailments through subtle changes in body language, voice or smell, experts say.[22]

Cats also can sense when humans are in despair or nearing the end of life. "Cats, like other animals, are very intuitive and can sense things that humans cannot. For example, their eyesight and sense of smell are more acute than ours," according to Michelle Prawirawidjaja, writing for the Emory WordPress blog *Anthropological Perspectives on Death*. She explained,

Because cats rely primarily on body language to communicate to one another, they must be attuned to biological and behavioral changes in the other animals around them. This includes detecting weakness or changes in body temperature and odor. They are also intuitive in that they often know when they are about to die. I have heard stories where cats hide or "run away" from home to find a place to pass away peacefully. Therefore, cats are attuned to their bodies and their environment to the point where they can detect signs associated with death.[23]

A rather famous black and white cat named Oscar has been the subject of numerous news and magazine stories about his ability to sense the imminent death of hospice patients, primarily those with Alzheimer's disease. Oscar lives in Steere House Nursing and Rehabilitation Center in Providence, Rhode Island. In 2015, David Raven reported in Mirror.co.uk that ten-year-old Oscar "is believed to have predicted the deaths of 100 people at a nursing home." Oscar "spends his

Watch It!

A Street Cat Named Bob is a comedy-drama film set in London, where James Bowen, a street busker (a person who performs in public places for donations) entertains. He wants a career as a professional musician, and to get a start he performs for audiences on the street. This film, released in 2016, is based on Bowen's autobiography of the same title published by Thomas Nunn Books/St. Martins Press in 2012. The story is about Bowen, a recovering addict who comes close to death when he overdoses on heroin. But his life begins to change when he adopts a stray ginger cat.

The first scenes depict Bowen, who is homeless and almost penniless, searching for food in alley dumpsters where rats scurry. He tries to buy food in a restaurant by literally singing for a meal but is kicked out. As the story progresses, Bowen and a friend, who is also homeless and an addict, find an unlocked parked car and get in to sleep. The owner of the car tries to evict the two addicts, but Bowen has overdosed on heroin and is unresponsive. His friend calls for an ambulance.

Bowen's drug counselor, Val, confronts him in the hospital and urges him to continue with a rehabilitation program and take the prescribed doses of methadone to help with withdrawal from drugs. Val finds an apartment for him, again asking that he promise to stick with the rehab program. In the apartment, Bowen has his first encounter with the tomcat, who has been able to sneak in to feed from an open box of cereal. After his first meeting with the cat, Bowen tries to find the feline's owner but fails. He discovers that the cat won't leave him and obviously intends to be Bowen's companion. The cat, now named Bob, follows Bowen to the streets for performances. Bob eventually becomes part of Bowen's street act and draws crowds and increased donations.

When Bowen finally kicks his addiction, he begins writing about his experiences with Bob and the development of their loving companionship. The film ends with Bowen's success as an author—or as coauthor with Bob the street cat, whose autograph is a paw print stamped alongside Bowen's name.

days roaming the halls of Steere House and is known by nurses for being notoriously anti-social." But that characteristic does not apply to dying people. The only residents the cat "cuddles up to are residents in their final dying days."[24]

David Dosa, MD, is assistant professor of medicine at Brown University. He studied Oscar's abilities and wrote a book about him, *Making the Rounds with Oscar: The Extraordinary Gift of an Ordinary Cat* published in 2010. The book has been highly praised and explains how the author learned to appreciate Oscar's ability to provide end-of-life care for patients and their families.

12

LIVING YOUR LIFE

··

"Wouldn't it be satisfying to say that you had no regrets and that you were pleased with how you lived your life?"—Kelley in ThisIBelieve.org[1]

As has been stated numerous times in this book: there is no doubt that one's time on planet Earth is limited. For some people that fact may convince them that they should live with reckless abandon and a YOLO (you only live once) attitude. Others may be inclined to approach life timidly and cautiously, afraid to venture forth and take risks. But facing the reality of death can also be a stimulator; you may be motivated to live as fully as possible without endangering or infringing on others. In other words, knowing that death is inevitable convinces many people to do their best to have a meaningful and fulfilling existence throughout their lifetime. The ancient Greek philosopher Epicurus noted that "the art of living well and dying well are one."[2]

Knowing that all humans die and that one's own death is inevitable allows many individuals to live in the present and appreciate the mundane things in life; to participate in activities of choice rather than just doing their duty; to create meaning in their lives. In short, they prioritize and are at peace with themselves.

In an essay for ThisIBelieve.org, a high school sophomore, Kelley of Madawaska, Maine, asked rhetorically, "Before you die wouldn't it be satisfying to say that you had no regrets and that you were pleased with how you lived your life? Looking back, you want to believe that every second you had was used to maximum potential, and that you enjoyed your life. I sure hope those are the thoughts going through my mind when I get older. But now is the time for me to make those memories and to live in the moment." She added, "If I am enjoying myself and staying safe and healthy while doing it, I think that is time well spent."[3]

Another teenager, Gini of Chester, Virginia, also wrote an essay for the same website. She noted, "I have always lived my life by trying to make the best of everything. Even if I make mistakes along the way, I do not regret any of them, because they have shaped me into becoming the person that I am today."[4]

Life Expectancy

Americans today can expect to live a certain number of years, depending on the date they were born and whether their health conditions at the time of birth remain the same throughout their lives. Life expectancy data, which change year by year, reflect the quality of health care in a particular nation and usually are related to socioeconomic factors. By comparing cross-cultural death and life expectancy rates, analysts can gauge social progress or can determine whether social inequalities are a factor in life expectancy rates.

Advances in medical technology, health care, and nutrition can add several months to life expectancy in an industrialized nation. Generally, the typical life span is longer in high-income nations than in low-income countries, and worldwide women generally live longer than men. (However, in some countries women are so repressed that they do not have adequate food and health care, which lowers their life expectancy.)

According to the Centers for Disease Control and Prevention, the ten leading causes of death in the United States in 2014 were (in order of occurrence, highest to lowest)

1. Heart disease
2. Cancer
3. Chronic lower respiratory diseases
4. Accidents (unintentional injuries)
5. Stroke (cerebrovascular diseases)
6. Alzheimer's disease
7. Diabetes
8. Influenza and pneumonia
9. Nephritis, nephrotic syndrome, and nephrosis [kidney problems]
10. Intentional self-harm (suicide)[5]

The *Washington Post* reported in February 2017 that life expectancy in the U.S. will be "83.3 years for women and 79.5 for men in 2030, up from 81.2 for women and 76.5 for men in 2010." However, the life span of Americans lags behind those of other wealthy countries, because in some parts of the United States people cannot afford health care, lack education about nutrition, and suffer high rates of homicide or suicide.[6]

Nevertheless, some scientists and medical researchers predict that young Americans born, say, in the year 2000, could live to be one hundred years old. That is no guarantee, of course, but you could reasonably expect to plan for many years of life ahead—if you have a healthy lifestyle and do not suffer a serious disease or injury.

Living Well

Advice for how to live well can be found in many books, countless blogs and articles on the Internet, sermons from religious leaders, your teachers, and certainly from your parents and other family members. Much advice focuses on such issues as eating nutritious foods, being physically fit, maintaining good mental health, continuing to learn, and sustaining personal relationships and making new friends.

There are even healthy lifestyle camps and various retreats to teach young people how to live in a religious/spiritual manner. "Living your best life requires you to maximize yourself mentally, physically, emotionally and spiritually," advises Celestine Chua, founder of a blog called *Personal Excellence*. She adds, "I always find living to be a fascinating experience. How we're all on earth, with millions of species, 30,000 different life forms, over 7 billion people, and all thriving in [their] own way, existing, co-existing and in co-creation mode. There's so much we don't know out there, so much to be experienced in life."[7]

Even though there is a lot to experience while we are alive, a long-term Harvard University study found that love is the key to a happy and fulfilling life. Beginning in 1938, the Harvard Grant Study followed a group of 268 male undergraduates for seventy-five years, among them President John F. Kennedy and former *Washington Post* editor Ben Bradlee. Although money and successful careers were certainly factors in a fulfilling life, the most important aspect was

Read It!

Get Out of Your Mind and Into Your Life for Teens: A Guide to Living an Extraordinary Life by Joseph Ciarrochi, Louise Hayes, and Ann Bailey is a paperback (New Harbinger, 2012) that can be helpful for teens struggling with fears, embarrassments, and other painful emotions. The publication is a workbook with skills that help young people cope with their inner turmoil. The book is divided into three parts, and the third section includes the chapters "Knowing What You Value," "Learning to Value Yourself," "Creating Friendship," "Seeking Your Way in The World," and "The Spark You Carry in Your Heart." By following the advice in the book, the authors expect readers to become strong, self-confident individuals who will be able to have a fulfilling life.

being connected in relationships, jobs, and other areas of life. "The Grant Study provides strong support for the growing body of research that has linked social ties with longevity, lower stress level, and improved overall well-being," wrote Caroline Gregoire for the *Huffington Post*.[8]

In a 2014 *Forbes* magazine article, contributor Karl Moore opined that for Millennials (young adults), "Money is important and they do enjoy making it, however, they long to be part of something bigger than themselves. The workplace doesn't define them to the degree that it did for too many Boomers [people born in the fifties]. Millennials want to lead a balanced life. They want to be happy at home and happy on the job—money is somewhat secondary."[9]

The Importance of Religion in People's Lives

When people acknowledge that their death is inevitable, they may or may not recognize the prominence of religion as it applies to living in a meaningful way before they die. Large numbers of Americans follow religious beliefs that advise living in a manner that will bring them spiritual strength and happiness until they die. As a Muslim teen living in England explained, "Being Muslim is what I am, it is my way of life. My faith is what helps me overcome my everyday problems. My faith gives me the right to live my life."[10]

Fizzah Abbasi, a student at George Mason University in Fairfax County, Virginia, expressed her views on how her Muslim faith has added meaning to her life. Writing in the *Huffington Post* blog in 2015, she explained, "When I started wearing the hijab a few months ago, I put my faith on display for everyone to see. I'm lucky to go to a university where there are many Muslims, but it still doesn't change the fact that we get treated differently at airports, or that our religion is constantly put on blast by the media." She lamented the fact that she often has "to convince people that no, my religion does not, in fact, support Al-Qaeda, or their more formidable successor, ISIS." She concluded,

> Living as a Muslim teen in America means taking all these unfair things and dealing with them. It means that whenever I walk outside with that scarf around my head, I am representing every Muslim in the world, and that everything I do reflects on an entire race of people. . . . None of this is simple, but I am willing to do anything for my faith and my beliefs, because without them, I have no idea who I am.[11]

Young people of other faiths also follow religious traditions because they believe that how they live has consequences throughout their time on Earth. For example, on the website EveryStudent.com, two young people shared how they found fulfillment, acceptance, and purpose in life through their Christian beliefs. One young woman, Marilyn A., who "came from an atheist background," noted,

> I have always thought that life should be meaningful. Not necessarily every moment of every day. I mean, how meaningful is it doing laundry? Nor should life always be serious. We all need extremely large doses of just having a good time! But life has to be more than pleasure-seeking, partly because the enjoyment doesn't last. It's here for a moment, then gone.[12]

Marilyn explained that she viewed God as a kind of Wizard of Oz, but studied many sources looking for fulfillment. "It amazed me that I could have a relationship with God. I talked to him and, through changes in circumstances, he indicated that he heard me. He led me in career paths that are far more expansive and exciting than I ever dreamed."[13]

In the Chicago area, students write and publish a weekly called the *Mash*, whose staff interviewed students in various area schools about the importance of religion in their lives. Among the interviewees was Sarah Weiner, who was a junior at Homewood-Flossmoor High School in 2015. In her words,

Research on Importance of Religion

More than half of Americans (53 percent) say that religion is important in their lives, the Pew Research Center reported. "And 40% of highly religious U.S. adults describe themselves as 'very happy,' compared with 29% of those who are less religious," a 2016 Pew Forum survey found. The survey defines "highly religious" as "those who pray daily and attend religious services at least once a week." The forum noted, "People who are highly religious are more engaged with their extended families, more likely to volunteer, more involved in their communities and generally happier with the way things are going in their lives" than those who are categorized as "not highly religious." In addition, the forum found that "nine-in-ten people who are categorized as highly religious (91%) say religion is very important in their lives, and nearly all the rest (7%) say religion is at least somewhat important to them. By contrast, only three-in-ten people who are classified as not highly religious (31%) say religion is very important in their lives, and most of the rest (38%) say religion is 'not too' or 'not at all' important to them."[a]

The Jewish faith is important to me because it gives me a sense of belonging and comfort that there is a higher power looking over me. . . . There are some strict rules that can go along with being Jewish, such as keeping kosher. I do not keep kosher, as a personal choice. I don't agree with the idea that you need to follow every little rule in the book to be a part of a faith. Not to say that I have anything against those who do keep kosher, it's just my personal choice.[14]

Madison Thompson, a student at Jones Prep School in Chicago, is a Buddhist and said, "Most days, I seek time to meditate, but that is more for my own state of mind rather than my religion, I guess. . . . I don't attend church or go to a temple."[15]

Haroon Ghiasudden, who was a junior at Islamic Foundation School in 2015, said in the *Mash* interview, "I am more traditional in my approach (to religion), but I find that it can still fit a contemporary lifestyle (or) setting." In other words modern life and faith can merge for Haroon, but he added, "My parents are pretty devout Muslims and have enrolled me in private Islamic schools that allowed me to get a religious and secular education. . . . Of course it's important to them that I'm religious, but it's as important to me."[16]

In another *Mash* interview Pedro Lagunas, a dedicated Catholic, told the student newspaper, "I grew up practicing this religion because I was forced to. . . . However, as I grew older, I became very interested in my religion and practice it a lot more often."[17]

Living a Meaningful Life as an Atheist or Agnostic

People of many religious faiths often ask atheists (nonbelievers) how they can have a good life and be prepared for death without God. The same question is directed to agnostics—those who are skeptical of religion and a divine being.

Kara, who identified herself as an atheist, explained that in high school she began to question the existence of God. When in her twenties, she decided it was not rational for her to believe in a deity. "I think we are immersed in a society that's pushing the idea of God in all these various and vague ways. . . . But, I don't see the proof," she argued. "I had this disbelief in spirituality and the existence of anything beyond the natural world. . . . No one was able to show me that spirituality existed. So I just accepted that there was no God."[18]

On the website of the Richard Dawkins Foundation, teenager Abby declared,

I'm an atheist. I happen to live in a very small, very religious town where I am somewhat notorious for my views. My family and I have been horribly harassed and outcasted. The biggest problem our religious neighbors seem to have is my age. I'm fifteen now and was only ten when I was ready to call myself an atheist. They tell my parents they raised me completely wrong and insist that I am simply too young to be atheistic. I have researched both science and theology. . . . I know more scripture than most Christians I know. I am not ignorant in the least. Besides, no one seems to have a problem with calling small children Christians and bringing them to church. Why is it any different? Should there be an age requirement to irreligiosity? Why are teen atheists or agnostics automatically deemed rebellious or ignorant?[19]

In 2016, Ryan Stringer, a graduate student at the University of California, San Diego, penned an article for the *Huffington Post* blog in which he stated that religion makes life meaningful for some people, but then noted, "Other people, like me, can't find any meaning in religion because they can't believe in it. So does this then mean that people like me can't have meaningful lives? Are our lives doomed to meaninglessness because they don't include religion?" His answer to both questions is a firm no. He wrote,

Life without religion can have purpose. We surely do need purpose in life in order to have a meaningful one; it's hard to imagine having a meaningful life without having a sense of purpose in it. And religion, of course, can provide such purpose for many people. Nevertheless, it would be a mistake to think that religion is needed for this purpose. . . . Religion doesn't have a monopoly on providing a sense of purpose in life. Instead, *we can give purpose to our own lives*. Taking care of our loved ones, helping needy humans or non-human animals, fighting for good causes (e.g., freedom and justice), striving for moral excellence, contributing to science, music, literature, art, or other areas of enduring human culture—such things can provide the non-religious with a sense of purpose in life.[20]

In a 2014 Religious Landscape Study, which was a follow-up to an earlier extensive study on religion, the Pew Research Center found that about 36 percent of Americans between the ages of eighteen and twenty-four (young Millennials) had no religious affiliation. About half of that group indicated "that a lack of belief led them to move away from religion. This includes many respondents who mention 'science' as the reason they do not believe in religious teachings, including one who said 'I'm a scientist now, and I don't believe in miracles.' Others reference 'common sense,' 'logic' or a 'lack of evidence'—or simply say they do not believe in God."[21]

Isaac Saul, an editor at the *Huffington Post* who has studied in Jerusalem, wrote,

> Truthfully, I haven't come to any conclusions of my own about the existence of God. . . . I'd say that I'm an agnostic. But I do that knowing that I pray frequently, sometimes try to talk to God (I still feel funny doing this), say blessings over kosher food, make traditional Shabbat kiddush every Friday night and do my best to eat a Shabbat dinner each week. Obviously, in these instances I'm subscribing to Judaism, and that's because it is the story of God I find most probable. The rest of my time I'm usually not thinking about God a whole ton, and I'm certainly not observing the many laws he's been said to have made. Still, I'm giving opportunities to each and discovering success in places I never thought I would.[22]

Living Life When Seriously Ill

Many young people who are chronically ill or who are facing their last days still try to go beyond the uncertainty of their lives. They try to live with as much happiness and fulfillment as possible. As one teenager put it,

> Treat us like any other teen would be treated. However, understand that we may not be able to do everything our peers do, and sometimes it might be hard for us to express how we feel when so many emotions just overwhelm us. It is hard for us to share with you exactly how we feel because most days we don't even know. We are not adults and we are certainly not children. It's certainly a crazy journey and it is not an easy one either. All I ask is that you treat us like any normal teenager, and are able to help us along the way but also give us some space. That's the only thing we truly want.[23]

To be treated and act like "any normal teenager," a young person with a chronic illness may decide, when possible, to continue everyday routines—perhaps playing in a school band, taking part in a play, serving as a volunteer for a charitable organization or political campaign. Certainly living with chronic illness can be stressful, but many young people try to learn as much as they can about their illness and treatment. They may also try new activities that make their lives enjoyable, such as photography, writing, art, and caring for animals.

Katherine Mitchell—a teenager with Marfan syndrome (a disorder that affects connective tissue), celiac disease (an autoimmune disease that requires a gluten-free diet), epilepsy, and heart disease—was not supposed to live beyond the age of fifteen. But in 2014 at the age of sixteen she was still living her life. For several years, she had a puppy named Roman that had the same diseases affecting Katherine. The puppy lived for only ten months, devastating Katherine. However, she decided to do something in memory of Roman and to fulfill her own life. She began volunteering at animal shelters, and "it soon became something more. She started Roman's Rescue, a non-profit to save animals scheduled to be put down at shelters," according to a report on LifewithDogs.tv. Katherine explained, "I want to start doing adoption events. I want to get bigger. . . . My dream is to get a TV show, like Pitbulls and Parolees or Pitboss, that's my dream." The article concludes by saying, " No one knows how much time Mitchell has left, but she is creating a legacy that will live on."[24]

Seventeen-year-old Simon Jones "is not interested in a story about what it's like to be dying. He is, however, game for telling a story about living. About living a normal life, a full life, a thrilling life, even a boring life, because boring can be a relief from the drama of a cancer called desmoplastic small round cell tumor," wrote Erin Grace in the *Omaha World-Herald* in November 2016. Simon has a Facebook page called "Simon Says: Live a Better Life." That life for Simon included a two-week adventure in September 2016 with his parents; his twenty-year-old sister; and his twelve-year-old brother. As reported in the *World-Herald*:

> Simon climbed mountains and rode river rapids in Colorado. He zip-lined in Utah. He climbed on high ropes in Arizona. He jumped off the Stratosphere Las Vegas, falling down, down, down, 108 stories down in the casino hotel's SkyJump. He surfed off the coast of California and hovered above a harbor in the Pacific Ocean, wearing a jetpack on one occasion. And jetboots on another. And in yet another thrill, Simon went sky diving. One glorious photo shows him grinning, arms outstretched as if hugging the blue California sky.[25]

In Simon's words, "Living a better life means bending but not breaking." It also "means striking a balance between honesty and inspiration."[26]

What Is a Meaningful Life?

Simon's definition of living a better life is certainly a good start for models to live by. But there is no single script for living a life that is meaningful, purposeful, and fulfilling. Each person has to find what really matters in life. A basic concept, as you probably know, is the biblical "do unto others as you would have them do unto you" or to put it another way: treat others as you want them to treat you.

In a *Scientific American* article, Matthew Hutson wrote,

Living well often involves helping a friend or relative find happiness, which in turn gives you meaning. © *iStock.com/Dobino*

As squishy as the concept sounds, meaning in life is an integral part of our well-being. Research has associated it with good mental health, success at work and longevity. Psychologists have proposed three aspects: significance, purpose and coherence. In other words, life is meaningful when it feels important, when it seems to have a point and when it makes sense.[27]

"Fulfillment is found by making a difference in the lives of others. Not only will you benefit others, over the long term you will find an increased sense of inner well-being. Your true merit is measured in how much you've mattered to others," according to Professor Susan Krauss Whitbourne at the University of Massachusetts, Amherst.[28]

Here are some simple suggestions that may help you in your pursuit for a fulfilling and meaningful lifetime.

- Keep your promises, which convinces others you are trustworthy and in turn adds to your feeling of self-regard.
- Appreciate and thank others for what they do for you. This, too, amplifies your self-esteem.
- Try not to concentrate on your mistakes; instead focus on your accomplishments.

- Look at obstacles as challenges—overcoming them boosts your morale and may be steps toward achieving a life goal.
- Volunteer for charity organizations or political campaigns whose missions align with your goals for a meaningful and purposeful life.

Finally, here's advice from former president Barack Obama in his January 20, 2017, farewell speech: "If you're tired of arguing with strangers on the Internet, try talking with one of them in real life. If something needs fixing, then lace up your shoes and do some organizing. If you're disappointed by your elected officials, grab a clipboard, get some signatures, and run for office yourself. Show up. Dive in. Stay at it."[29]

Appendix: Sample of Advance Care Directive

Doctors and lawyers recommend that young adults (eighteen years old and older) complete an advance care directive regarding their health care in case of unexpected end-of-life situations (such as a fatal car accident) or terminal illness. If you are in a situation where you cannot speak for yourself, advance care directives spell out your wishes about health care and who should advocate on your behalf. No one is legally required to complete these documents, but portions of Advance Care Directive for Florida are included here as *samples only*. The sample document is meant to provide information about the content of such a directive. The information is not copyrighted and was made available free of charge online by Lifecare Directives, LLC at www.lifecaredirectives.com or contact them at 5348 Vegas Drive #11, Las Vegas, Nevada, 89108; phone: 877–559–0527. (Other state forms are also available on the Lifecare Directives website.)

Important Notice:

An advance directive is not a substitute for medical, legal or other necessary advice or direction. This document should not be construed as offering counseling, medical, legal, financial, or estate planning or advice, nor any other similar guidance or direction. Such counsel should be obtained from qualified, certified, and licensed professionals in your locale who are experienced in the specific areas of concern. Completion of this document constitutes acceptance of its content both in whole and in part, as well as a determination of its utility for the purposes indicated.

Lifecare Directives, LLC, and all involved in this document's design, publication, and distribution assume no liability for its use, including that which may arise from omissions, technical inaccuracies, and typographical errors. Diligent efforts notwithstanding, this document is not warrantied to be in compliance with state and local laws. All warranties, including those of merchantability, fitness for a particular purpose, and non-infringement are expressly disclaimed. The utilizer agrees to seek appropriate outside review prior to completion. The utilizer and all heirs, assigns, designees, devisees, representatives, and all others involved, agree to assume all liability for its use and any subsequent outcomes, and to release and hold harmless all involved in its design, publication, advertising and distribution. The utilizer also agrees that any physician, health care provider, agent, proxy, surrogate, representative, mediator, court officer, and all others relying on the document's content are similarly free of all liability, when they act in good faith and with due diligence to follow the recorded wishes and directions. . . .

Understanding Your Directive:

This directive is written in three parts. While it is best if you fill out the entire document, you may choose to complete only Section I, which is a living will, through which you may leave a statement of your wishes. Or, you may choose to complete only Section II, which is a declaration of your desires to be an organ and tissue donor. Or you may complete only Section III, which is a Health Care Surrogate designation by which to name someone to speak for you if you ever become unable to speak for yourself. Ideally, you will complete all three sections to ensure that your wishes are known and that you are represented as fully as possible.

SECTION I: FLORIDA LIVING WILL DECLARATION

(Pursuant to Florida Statute §765.303)
Declaration made this _____ day of _____, 20_____,
Be it known that I, _____,
Print Full Name Date of Birth _____
willfully and voluntarily make known my desire that my dying not be artificially prolonged under the circumstances set forth below, and I do hereby declare that, if at any time I am incapacitated and (initial as applicable):
_____ I have a terminal condition
_____ I have an end-stage condition
_____ I am in a persistent vegetative state
and if my attending or treating physician and another consulting physician have determined that there is no reasonable medical probability of my recovery from such condition, I direct that life-prolonging procedures be withheld or withdrawn when the application of such procedures would serve only to prolong artificially the process of dying, and that I be permitted to die naturally with only the administration of medication or the performance of any

medical procedure deemed necessary to provide me with comfort care or to alleviate pain.

It is my intention that this declaration be honored by my family and physician as the final expression of my legal right to refuse medical or surgical treatment and to accept the consequences for such refusal. I understand the full import of this declaration, and I am emotionally and mentally competent to make this declaration.

Additional instructions (optional): _____

Signature: _____

Full Name: _____

Signed: _____

Date: _____

Required Witnesses:

(at least one of the witnesses must not be a spouse or blood relative)

Signature: _____

Printed Name: _____

Address: _____

Signature: _____

Printed Name: _____

Address: _____

SECTION II: ANATOMICAL GIFT DECLARATION

(Pursuant to Florida Statute §765.514)

Full Name: _____

Be it Known that I hereby make this anatomical gift, if medically acceptable, to take effect upon my death. The words and marks below indicate my desires (initial as applicable):

_____ Any needed organs or parts for the purpose of transplantation, therapy, medical research, or education.

_____ Only the following organs or parts:

Specify: _____

_____ My entire body for anatomical study, if needed (requires prior arrangements with a medical school, university, or other approved institution)

Limitations, Special Wishes, Other Concerns: _____

_____

Donor Signature: _____

Required Witnesses:

(at least one of the witnesses must not be a spouse or blood relative)

1.

Signature: _____

Printed Name: _____

Address: _____

2.

Signature: _____

Printed Name: _____

Address: _____

SECTION III: DESIGNATION OF HEALTH CARE SURROGATE

(Pursuant to Florida Statute §765.203)

Full Name: _____

Be It Known That:

In the event that I have been determined to be incapacitated to provide informed consent for medical treatment and surgical and diagnostic procedures, I wish to designate as my surrogate for health care decisions: _____

_____

If my surrogate is unwilling or unable to perform his or her duties, I wish to designate as

my alternate surrogate:

Alternate: _____

Address: _____

Telephone: Home: _____ Work: _____

Cell Phone or Pager: _____ E-mail: _____

I fully understand that this designation will permit my designee to make health care decisions, except for anatomical gifts, unless I have executed an anatomical gift declaration pursuant to law (above), and to provide, withhold, or withdraw consent on my behalf; to apply for public benefits to defray the cost of health care; and to authorize my admission to or transfer from a health care facility.

Additional instructions (optional): _____

_____

I further affirm that this designation is not being made as a condition of treatment or admission to a health care facility. I will notify and send a copy of this document to the following persons other than my surrogate, so they may know who my surrogate is.

Name: _____

Address: _____

Name: _____

Address: _____

Signature: _____

Full Name: _____

Signed: _____

Date: _____

Required Witnesses:

(at least one of the witnesses must not be a spouse or blood relative)

1.

Signature: _____

Printed Name: _____

Address: _____

2.

Signature: _____

Printed Name: _____

Address: _____

Glossary

advance directive: document with instructions for medical care if terminally or seriously ill

apocalypse: cataclysmic destruction of evil in order to raise up a righteous kingdom

autopsy: opening up and dissecting a corpse

bequest: gift or donation

bereavement: mourning

bier: platform for cremation

brain dead: loss of all brain function

caisson: horse-pulled wagon carrying remains of honored military dead

casket: container for burying a corpse; also known as a coffin

catacomb: tomb for deceased

condolences: sympathy for grieving persons

coroner: official who investigates cause of a death

corpse: dead body

cortege: funeral procession

cremation: disposing a body by burning

crypt: underground tomb or burial place, often beneath a church

embalm: preserve a body with chemical or herbal injections

endowment: gift specified for an individual, organization, or religious institution upon a person's death

epidemic: widespread disease

epitaph: an engraving on a gravestone or statement memorializing a deceased person

eulogy: written or oral commentary honoring the deceased

euphemism: rewording in order to soften harshness of a term

euthanasia: allowing or helping a terminally ill patient or domestic animal to die

exhumation: unearthing human remains

fetus: developing form after conception

genocide: systematic murder of a racial or ethnic group

ghost: manifestation of a dead person

gravestone: marker to identify a grave in a cemetery or other burial place

hearse: vehicle to transport a body

hieroglyphics: form of ancient writing with symbols

Hippocratic Oath: pledge made by medical doctors

hospice: care for seriously or terminally ill people with focus on pain management and emotional and spiritual support

karma: consequences that determine a person's existence after reincarnation

mausoleum: large stone tomb for the dead

obituary: published notice of a person's death

palliative care: managing a patient's needs, physical pain, emotional suffering, and religious concerns

pandemic: widespread disease that results in the death of huge numbers of people

probate: legal process that usually involves filing a deceased person's will

reincarnation: rebirth after death

soul: essence of a person

spirit: continuation of a person in afterlife

thanatology: scientific study of death and its social, psychological, legal, and moral aspects

vigil: standing watch

Notes

Chapter 1

1. Jocelyn, "Fear of Dying," TeenHelp.org, July 14, 2011, http://www.teenhelp.org/forums/f3-general/t79267-fear-dying/ (accessed January 15, 2017).
2. Female in California, "Fear of Dying," TeenHelp.org, July 14, 2011, http://www.teenhelp.org/forums/f3-general/t79267-fear-dying/ (accessed September 25, 2016).
3. Jake, "Fear of Dying," TeenHelp.org, October 6, 2010, http://www.teenhelp.org/forums/f3-general/t79267-fear-dying/ (accessed September 25, 2016).
4. Salli Rasberry and Carole Rae Watanabe, *The Art of Dying: Honoring and Celebrating Life's Passages* (Berkeley, CA: Celestial Arts, 2001), 160.
5. Lisa Fritscher, "Phasmophobia—Fear of Ghosts Treatment, VeryWell.com, updated September 6, 2016, https://www.verywell.com/phasmophobia-2671876 (accessed September 25, 2016); see the section titled "Thanatophobia."
6. Robert Kastenbaum, "Children and Adolescents' Understanding of Death," Death Reference.com, n.d., http://www.deathreference.com/Ce-Da/Children-and-Adolescents-Understanding-of-Death.html (accessed September 24, 2016).
7. James Rainey, "Unseen Pictures, Untold Stories: How the U.S. Press Has Sanitized the War in Iraq," DemocracyNow.org, May 24, 2005, http://www.democracynow.org/2005/5/24/unseen_pictures_untold_stories_how_the (accessed October 26, 2016).
8. Elliot Essman, "Death in the USA," LifeintheUSA.com, 2014, http://www.lifeintheusa.com/death/index.html (accessed September 22, 2016).
9. Essman, "Death in the USA."
10. U.S. Department of Veterans Affairs, "America's Wars," VA.gov, May 2016, https://www.va.gov/opa/publications/factsheets/fs_americas_wars.pdf (accessed February 27, 2017).
11. Civil War Trust, "Civil War Facts," CivilWar.org, 2014, http://www.civilwar.org/education/history/faq/ (accessed November 14, 2016).
12. Mayo Clinic Staff, "Living Wills and Advance Directives for Medical Decisions," MayoClinic.org, n.d., http://www.mayoclinic.org/healthy-lifestyle/consumer-health/in-depth/living-wills/art-20046303 (accessed September 23, 2016).
13. Charles A. Corr and Donna M. Corr, *Learning about Death, Dying, and Bereavement*, 7th ed. (Belmont, CA: Wadsworth Cengage Living, 2013), 14.
14. Corr and Corr, *Learning about Death*, 13.
15. Jessica Nutik Zitter, "First, Sex Ed. Then Death Ed.," *New York Times*, February 18, 2017, https://www.nytimes.com/2017/02/18/opinion/sunday/first-sex-ed-then-death-ed.html?_r=0 (accessed March 15, 2017).
16. Zitter, "First, Sex Ed."

a. See the Death Cafe website at http://deathcafe.com/what/ (accessed March 27, 2017).

b. Deena Prichep, "Death Cafes Breathe Life into Conversations about Dying," NPR.org, March 8, 2013, http://www.npr.org/2013/03/08/173808940/death-cafes-breathe-life-into -conversations-about-dying (accessed December 13, 2016).

c. Prichep, "Death Cafes Breathe Life."

Chapter 2

1. See "Teen Grief: Mourning the Death of a Friend," *Grief Healing* (blog), n.d., http://www .griefhealingblog.com/2015/10/teen-grief-mourning-death-of-friend.html (accessed February 28, 2017).

2. See "Teen Grief: Mourning the Death of a Parent," *Grief Healing* (blog), n.d., http://www .griefhealingblog.com/2011/07/teen-grief-mourning-death-of-parent.html (accessed February 28, 2017).

3. Zach, "When A Friend Dies by Suicide," SPTSUSA.org, n.d., http://www.sptsusa.org/teens/ when-a-friend-dies-by-suicide/ (accessed October 26, 2016).

4. See Centers for Disease Control and Prevention, "Teen Drivers: Get the Facts," CDC.gov, n.d., https://www.cdc.gov/motorvehiclesafety/teen_drivers/teendrivers_factsheet.html (accessed February 1, 2017).

5. Erika Bazaldua, "Friends of Second Harmony Teen Who Died after Crash Share Stories, Memories," KLTV.com, June 7, 2016, http://www.kltv.com/story/32168899/friends-of-second -harmony-teen-who-died-after-crash-share-stories-memories (accessed October 27, 2016).

6. See Arialdi M. Miniño, "Mortality among Teenagers Aged 12–19 Years: United States, 1999–2006," *NCHS Data Brief*, no. 37 (May 2010), https://www.cdc.gov/nchs/data/databriefs/ db37.pdf (accessed November 3, 2016).

7. See "Key Gun Violence Statistics," BradyCampaign.org, n.d., http://www.bradycampaign .org/key-gun-violence-statistics (accessed January 28, 2017).

8. See http://www.azlyrics.com/lyrics/zachsobiech/clouds.html; see also https://www.youtube .com/watch?v=3HtCXgo4fvU (accessed March 10, 2017).

9. Kalhan Rosenblatt, "Friends of Girl, 18, with Leukemia Sign Her Casket with Loving Messages in a Final Goodbye after She Died Waiting for a Hospital Bed during a Shortage in Canada," *Daily Mail*, February 6, 2016, updated February 8, 2016, http://www.dailymail .co.uk/news/article-3435131/Friends-girl-18-leukemia-sign-casket-loving-messages-final -goodbye-died-waiting-hospital-bed-shortage-Canada.html (accessed February 1, 2017).

10. National Eating Disorders Association, "Get the Facts on Eating Disorders," NationalEating Disorders.org, n.d., https://www.nationaleatingdisorders.org/get-facts-eating-disorders (accessed November 5, 2016).

11. Bridget Ortigao, "After Daughter's Death, Longview Woman Plans to Educate about Eating Disorders," *Longview News-Journal*, March 1, 2015, https://www.news-journal.com/ news/2015/mar/01/i-still-get-to-be-her-mom/ (accessed November 5, 2016).

12. David Mccormack, "Girl, 15, Dies from Heart Attack Brought On by Eating Disorder That Started When Classmate Said Her 'Butt Looked Big' in Volleyball Shorts," *Daily Mail*, March 1, 2015, updated March 2, 2015, http://www.dailymail.co.uk/news/article-2974929/ Girl-15-dies-heart-attack-brought-eating-disorder-started-classmate-said-butt-looked-big -volleyball-shorts.html (accessed November 3, 2016).

13. Elisabeth Kübler-Ross, *On Death and Dying* (New York: Macmillan, 2007), 275.

14. Molly Clever and David R. Segal, "The Demographics of Military Children and Families," *Future of Children* 23, no. 2 (Fall 2013), http://www.futureofchildren.org/sites/futureof children/files/media/military_children_and_families_23_02_fulljournal.pdf (accessed May 15, 2017).

15. Abigail H. Gewirtz, Christopher R. Erbes, Melissa A. Polusny, Marion S. Forgatch, and David S. DeGarmo, "Helping Military Families through the Deployment Process: Strategies to Support Parenting," NCBI, August 12, 2011, https://www.ncbi.nlm.nih.gov/pmc/articles/ PMC3155511/ (accessed November 5, 2016).

16. National Military Family Association, "10 Things Military Kids Want You to Know," MilitaryFamily.org, n.d., accessed at http://drugfreeazkids.org/sites/default/files/10%20 things%20article-NMFA09.pdf (accessed February 28, 2017).

17. National Military Family Association, "10 Things Military Kids Want You to Know."

18. Allison K. Holmes, Paula K. Rauch, and Colonel Stephen J. Cozza (retired), "When a Parent Is Injured or Killed in Combat," *Future of Children* 23, no. 2 (Fall 2013), p. 152, http:// www.futureofchildren.org/sites/futureofchildren/files/media/military_children_and_families _23_02_fulljournal.pdf (accessed May 15, 2017).

19. Clever and Segal, "The Demographics of Military Children and Families."

20. Ian Shapira, "A Stranger's Tribute," *Washington Post*, January 1, 2015, http://www .washingtonpost.com/sf/childrenofthefallen/2015/01/05/jordan-phaneuf-17-a-strangers -message/ (accessed November 7, 2016).

21. Steve Hendrix, "New Ways to Mourn," *Washington Post*, January 5, 2015, http://www .washingtonpost.com/sf/childrenofthefallen/2015/01/05/leah-andrews-19-new-ways-to -mourn/ (accessed November 7, 2016).

22. Steve Hendrix, "Children of the Fallen: Portraits of Loss," *Washington Post*, 2015, http:// www.washingtonpost.com/sf/childrenofthefallen/story/portraits/ (accessed November 8, 2016).

---

a. Marty Tousley, "Teen Grief: Mourning the Death of a Friend," *Grief Healing* (blog), October 2015, http://www.griefhealingblog.com/2015/10/teen-grief-mourning-death-of-friend.html (accessed January 28, 2017).

b. Marty Tousley, "Teen Grief: Mourning the Death of a Parent," *Grief Healing* (blog), July 2011, http://www.griefhealingblog.com/2011/07/teen-grief-mourning-death-of-parent.html (accessed January 28, 2017).

c. See Barack Obama, "Presidential Proclamation—Military Family Month, 2016," The White House, October 27, 2016, https://obamawhitehouse.archives.gov/the-press-office/2016/10/27/ presidential-proclamation-military-family-month-2016 (accessed February 28, 2017).

Chapter 3

1. Kimberly Houghton, "In Nashua, Teens Hold a Vigil for Lost Friend," *Union Leader*, October 26, 2016, http://www.unionleader.com/safety/In-Nashua-teens-hold-a-vigil-for-lost -friend-10262016 (accessed January 15, 2017).

2. Caitlin Mota, "Jersey City Teens Hold Vigil for Classmate Killed by Cop's Son," *Jersey Journal*, September 20, 2016, http://www.nj.com/jjournal-news/index.ssf/2016/09/jersey_city _teens_hold_vigil_f.html (accessed November 9, 2016).

3. Kelley Hoskins, "Vigil for Murdered 14-Year-Old at Fairground Park," Fox2Now.com, October 28, 2016, http://fox2now.com/2016/10/28/vigil-for-murdered-14-year-old-at-fair grounds-park/ (accessed November 12, 2016).

4. See American Counseling Association, "Coping in the Aftermath of a Shooting," Counseling .org, n.d., https://www.counseling.org/knowledge-center/coping-in-the-aftermath-of-a -shooting (accessed November 11, 2016).

5. See "Change of the Guard," ArlingtonCemetery.mil, n.d., http://www.arlingtoncemetery .mil/Explore/Changing-of-the-Guard (accessed November 9, 2016).

6. Allan Guttmacher Institute, "U.S. Teen Pregnancy, Birth and Abortion Rates Reach the Lowest Levels in Almost Four Decades," news release, Guttmacher.org, April 5, 2016, https://www.guttmacher.org/news-release/2016/us-teen-pregnancy-birth-and-abortion -rates-reach-lowest-levels-almost-four-decades (accessed March 1, 2017).

7. "32 States with the Death Penalty and 18 States with Death Penalty Bans," ProCon.org, May 3, 2013, last updated December 9, 2016, http://deathpenalty.procon.org/view.resource .php?resourceID=001172 (accessed March 1, 2017).

8. "Penn State York Students Hold Vigil for Peace," news release, *Penn State News*, November 24, 2015, http://news.psu.edu/story/382426/2015/11/24/campus-life/penn-state-york -students-hold-vigil-peace (accessed November 15, 2016).

9. "Penn State York Students Hold Vigil for Peace."

10. "Penn State York Students Hold Vigil for Peace."

11. Lee V. Gaines, "Dozens Attend Interfaith Peace Vigil in Morton Grove," *Chicago Tribune*, June 6, 2016, http://www.chicagotribune.com/suburbs/morton-grove/news/ct-mgc-morton -grove-peace-vigil-tl-0609-20160606-story.html (accessed November 15, 2016).

12. Courtney Wheaton, "Local Group of Teens Spearhead Community Wide Prayer Vigil," WSET.com, July 21, 2016, http://wset.com/news/local/local-group-of-teens-spearhead -community-wide-prayer-vigil (accessed March 1, 2017).

13. Elizabeth Tyree, "Boys with a Dream Enjoys Their Two Days in Washington, DC," WSET. com, September 14, 2016, http://wset.com/news/local/boys-with-a-dream-enjoys-their-two -days-in-washington-dc (accessed March 1, 2017).

---

a. Brady Campaign to Prevent Gun Violence, "Key Gun Violence Statistics," BradyCampaign .org, 2016, http://www.bradycampaign.org/key-gun-violence-statistics (accessed November 15, 2016).

b. See John Vettese, "Speak Out," *Student Voices*, September 26, 2011, retrieved from AnnenbergClassroom.org, http://www.annenbergclassroom.org/speakout/is-the-death-penalty -constitutional (accessed November 15, 2016).

c. Sierra Watts, "Class Debate Inspires Death Penalty Opinion," *Raider Reader*, March 17, 2016, http://www.raiderreader.org/death-penalty/ (accessed November 11, 2016).

d. Michael F., "The Death Penalty," *Teen Ink*, n.d., http://www.teenink.com/opinion/all/ article/11085/The-Death-Penalty/ (accessed January 6, 2017).

Chapter 4

1. Chris Togneri, "Terminal Cancer Doesn't Stop High School Sweethearts from Making Vows," TribLive.com, February 27, 2016, http://triblive.com/news/projects/ourstories/10024010-74/ luke-natalie-cancer (accessed March 2, 2017).

2. National Cancer Institute, "Adolescents and Young Adults with Cancer," Cancer.gov, May 15, 2015, https://www.cancer.gov/types/aya (accessed November 27, 2016).

3. Bill Briggs, "Connecticut Teen with Curable Cancer Must Continue Chemo: Court," NBC News.com, January 8, 2015, http://www.nbcnews.com/health/cancer/connecticut-teen -curable-cancer-must-continue-chemo-court-n282421 (accessed December 2, 2016).

4. Togneri, "Terminal Cancer."

5. WPXI Pittsburgh, "Canonsburg Teen Who Inspired So Many Loses Battle with Terminal Cancer," WPXI.com, August 8, 2016, http://www.wpxi.com/news/canonsburg-teen -battling-terminal-cancer-graduates-from-high-school/330443074 (accessed November 27, 2016)

6. Max Edwards, "I'm 16. Five Months Ago, I Was Diagnosed with Terminal Cancer," *Guardian*, March 19, 2016, https://www.theguardian.com/lifeandstyle/2016/mar/19/im-16-five -months-ago-i-was-diagnosed-with-terminal-cancer?CMP=fb_gu (accessed December 1, 2016).

7. Edwards, "I'm 16."

8. "Deadly Diseases: Epidemics Through History," CNN.com, October 2014, http://www.cnn .com/interactive/2014/10/health/epidemics-through-history/ (accessed November 25, 2016).

9. Richard Knox, "2009 Flu Pandemic Was 10 Times More Deadly Than Previously Thought," NPR.org, November 26, 2013, http://www.npr.org/sections/health-shots/ 2013/11/26/247379604/2009-flu-pandemic-was-10-times-more-deadly-than-previously- thought (accessed March 2, 2017).

10. Daniel J. DeNoon and Miranda Hitti, "Swine Flu FAQ," WebMD.com, n.d., http://www .webmd.com/cold-and-flu/features/swine-flu-faq-1#2 (accessed March 2, 2017).

11. Zappyext, "In Remembrance of Carly Christenson," YouTube.com, January 9, 2013, https:// www.youtube.com/watch?v=yezrRQwxSpY (accessed March 2, 2017).

12. Jodi Whitworth, "Iowa Teenager Dies Days after Flu Symptoms Appear," WHOtv.com, January 2, 2015, http://whotv.com/2015/01/02/iowa-teenager-dies-days-after-flu-symptoms -appear/ (accessed March 2, 2017).

13. Ann Harding, "The 9 Deadliest Viruses on Earth," *Live Science*, October 27, 2016, http:// www.livescience.com/56598-deadliest-viruses-on-earth.html (accessed November 26, 2016).

14. See "Ryan White Quotes," BrainyQuite.com, n.d., https://www.brainyquote.com/quotes/ authors/r/ryan_white.html (accessed March 2, 2017).

15. Centers for Disease Control and Prevention, "HIV among Youth in the US," CDC.gov, April 27, 2016, http://www.cdc.gov/hiv/pdf/group/age/youth/cdc-hiv-youth.pdf (accessed November 25, 2016).

16. Mina, "Meet Mina, a Teen Living with HIV," PWN-USA.org, April 9, 2015, https://pwnusa .wordpress.com/2015/04/09/meet-mina-a-teen-living-with-hiv/ (accessed November 25, 2016).

17. Mina, "Meet Mina."

18. Clara Ritger, "Teen Hopes Her Story of Living with HIV Helps Others," *USA Today*, June 22, 2013, http://www.usatoday.com/story/news/nation/2013/06/22/teen-hopes-her-story-of -living-with-hiv-helps-others/2449457/ (accessed November 25, 2016).

19. Ritger, "Teen Hopes Her Story."

20. Paige Rawl, "Spotlight: Paige Rawl," GirlsHealth.gov, March 4, 2015, https://www .girlshealth.gov/spotlight/2015/3.html (accessed November 30, 2016).

21. See "Who We Are," WhatWorksinYouthHIV.org, n.d., https://www.whatworksinyouthhiv .org/who-we-are (accessed November 30, 2016).

a. Sally C. Curtin, Arialdi M. Miniño, and Robert N. Anderson, Centers for Disease Control and Prevention, "Declines in Cancer Death Rates among Children and Adolescents in the United States, 1999–2014," *NCHS Data Brief*, no. 257 (September 2016), http://www.cdc.gov/nchs/data/databriefs/db257.pdf (accessed November 30, 2016).

b. Dr. Howard Markel, "Remembering Ryan White, the Teen Who Fought the Stigma of AIDS," PBS.org, April 8, 2016, http://www.pbs.org/newshour/updates/remembering-ryan-white-the-teen-who-fought-against-the-stigma-of-aids/ (accessed November 27, 2016).

c. See Health Resources and Services Administration, "Ryan White HIV/AIDS Program Legislation," HRSA.gov, n.d., http://hab.hrsa.gov/about-ryan-white-hivaids-program/ryan-white-hivaids-program-legislation (accessed November 30, 2016).

Chapter 5

1. Rachel Premak, "'I'm Going to Be Free': Terminally Ill Wisconsin Teen Schedules Her Death and One 'Last Dance,'" *Washington Post*, July 21, 2016, https://www.washingtonpost.com/news/morning-mix/wp/2016/07/21/one-last-dance-for-this-wisconsin-teen-who-has-scheduled-her-own-death/?utm_term=.71bb952a311e (accessed January 18, 2017).

2. Jan Hoffman, "Teenagers Face Early Death, on Their Terms," *Well* (*New York Times* blog), March 28, 2015, http://well.blogs.nytimes.com/2015/03/28/teen-advance-directive-end-of-life-care/?_r=0 (accessed September 24, 2016).

3. Hoffman, "Teenagers Face Early Death."

4. See http://medical-dictionary.thefreedictionary.com/death+with+dignity (accessed December 3, 2016).

5. See http://www.finalexitnetwork.org/ (accessed December 5, 2016).

6. Compassion and Choices, *About Compassion and Choices*, brochure, April 5, 2016, p. 2, https://www.compassionandchoices.org/wp-content/uploads/2016/02/About-Compassion-and-Choices-Brochure-FINAL-4.05.16-Approved-for-Public-Distribution.pdf (accessed December 3, 2016)

7. Get Palliative Care, "Living Well with Serious Illness: Aly's Palliative Care Story," *Get Palliative Blog*, August 2016, https://getpalliativecare.org/living-well-serious-illness-alys-palliative-care-story/ (accessed May 15, 2017).

8. Get Palliative Care, "Living Well with Serious Illness."

9. Cristy Kern, "Buffalo Teen Creates Bucket List after Receiving Devastating Diagnosis," WIVB.com, last updated November 8, 2016, http://wivb.com/2016/11/07/buffalo-teen-creates-bucket-list-after-receiving-devastating-diagnosis/ (accessed March 3, 2017).

10. Ann Villet-Lagomarsino (reprint from Educational Broadcasting Corporation/Public Affairs Television, Inc.), "The Differences between Hospice and Palliative Care," Caregivers Library.org, 2016, http://www.caregiverslibrary.org/caregivers-resources/grp-end-of-life-issues/hsgrp-hospice/hospice-vs-palliative-care-article.aspx (accessed December 6, 2016).

11. Hospice of the Valley, "Teen Volunteer Testimonials," HOV.org, n.d., https://www.hov.org/teen-volunteer-programs (accessed December 6, 2016).

12. Hospice of the Valley, "Teen Volunteer Testimonials."

13. See "Stories," MontgomeryHospice.org, http://www.montgomeryhospice.org/volunteer/volunteer-stories (accessed December 6, 2016).

14. Ebony Faber, "Where Are They Now? Hospice Teen Volunteers—Turned—Nurses Q&A," EmpathHealth.org, September 9, 2016, https://empathhealth.org/6591-2/ (accessed February 2, 2017).

15. Faber, "Where Are They Now?"

16. Nessa Coyle, "Palliative Care, Hospice Care, and Bioethics: A Natural Fit," *Journal of Hospice and Palliative Nursing* 16, no. 1 (February 2014), http://journals.lww.com/jhpn/Fulltext/2014/02000/Palliative_Care,_Hospice_Care,_and_Bioethics__A.3.aspx (accessed January 31, 2017).

17. Alan Meisel, JD, "End of Life Care," TheHastingsCenter.org, n.d., http://www.thehastings center.org/briefingbook/end-of-life-care/ (accessed January 31, 2017).

a. Aimee Swartz, "Back from the Brain-Dead," *Newsweek*, May 6, 2016, pp. 36–38. Also "Brain Imaging Scans Show Some Vegetative Patients Are Living on the Edge of Consciousness," *Newsweek*, April 26, 2016, http://www.newsweek.com/2016/05/06/vegetative-state -consciousness-brain-imaging-452747.html (accessed February 2, 2017).

b. Jim Collar, "Appleton Teen Makes Heartbreaking Decision to Die," *Post-Crescent*, July 14, 2016, http://www.postcrescent.com/story/news/2016/07/14/appleton-teen-makes-heart breaking-decision-die/86510526/ (accessed May 15, 2017).

c. Jim Collar, "Jerika Bolen Dies after Ceasing Treatment," *Post-Crescent*, September 22, 2016, http://www.postcrescent.com/story/news/2016/09/22/jerika-bolen-dies-after-ceasing -treatment/90848584/ (accessed December 2, 2016).

d. See Sara Vallone, "After Sick Teen Ends Her Life, Mom Has Words for Critics Questioning Why She Let Her Daughter Die," *Independent Journal Review*, September 2016, http://ijr .com/2016/09/699567-after-sick-teen-ends-her-life-mom-has-words-for-critics-questioning -why-she-let-her-daughter-die/ (accessed January 18, 2017).

Chapter 6

1. Erika P., "A Free Will to Die," *Teen Ink*, n.d., https://www.teenink.com/opinion/all/article/10828/A-Free-Will-To-Die/ (accessed January 25, 2017).

2. "Attitudes towards Assisted Dying," *Economist*, June 27, 2015, http://www.economist.com/news/briefing/21656121-idea-whose-time-has-come-attitudes-towards-assisted-dying (accessed February 2, 2017).

3. Sean B., "Euthanasia," *Teen Ink*, n.d., http://www.teenink.com/opinion/all/article/10709/Euthanasia/ (accessed November 23, 2016).

4. Erika P., "A Free Will to Die."

5. Sarah Klammer, "A Teen's Thoughts on Euthanasia," ChristianLifeResources.com, 2011, http://www.christianliferesources.com/article/a-teen-s-thoughts-on-euthanasia-1445 (accessed March 3, 2017).

6. Kara, "The Case against Euthanasia and Doctor-Assisted Suicide," GenerationsforLife.org, May 23, 2011, http://generationsforlife.org/2011/0523/the-case-against-euthanasia-and -doctor-assisted-suicide/ (accessed March 3, 2017).

7. Katie Delach, "Despite Increasing Global Legalization of Physician-Assisted Suicide, Use Remains Rare, Penn Study Finds," news release, PennMedicine.org, July 5, 2016, http://www.uphs.upenn.edu/news/News_Releases/2016/07/emanuel/ (accessed March 4, 2017).

8. Delach, "Despite Increasing."

a. See AP, "Chile's President Visits Teen Who Asked to Die," CBSNews.com, February 28, 2015, http://www.cbsnews.com/news/chile-president-michelle-bachelet-visits-valentina -maureira-teen-who-asked-to-die/ (accessed March 3, 2017).
b. See Peter Tyson, "The Hippocratic Oath Today," PBS.org, March 27, 2001, http://www.pbs .org/wgbh/nova/body/hippocratic-oath-today.html (accessed November 23, 2016).
c. See *Bouvia v. Superior Court* on the Harvard website, https://h2o.law.harvard.edu/cases/4122 (accessed January 30, 2017).

Chapter 7

1. Substance Abuse and Mental Health Services Administration (SAMHSA), *A Journey toward Health and Hope: Your Handbook for Recovery After a Suicide Attempt* (Rockville, MD: U.S. Department of Health and Human Services, 2015), 4, http://www.suicidology.org/Portals/14/docs/ Resources/HandbookForRecoveryAfterAttemptSAMHSA.pdf (accessed January 15, 2017).
2. Centers for Disease Control and Prevention, National Center for Health Statistics, "Suicide and Self-Inflicted Injury," CDC.gov, last updated October 6, 2016, http://www.cdc.gov/nchs/ fastats/suicide.htm (accessed November 18, 2016).
3. Emma Margolin, "Adolescent Suicide Spike Leaving Families in Agony," NBCNews.com, December 5, 2016, http://www.nbcnews.com/news/us-news/suicide-14-i-have-racked-my -brain-trying-understand-n686036 (accessed March 4, 2017).
4. Leonard Pitts, "The Lonely Death of Naika Venant," *Tampa Bay Times*, January 29, 2017, p. 3P.
5. Patrick Farrell, "Another Girl Hangs Herself While Streaming It Live—This Time in Miami," *Miami Herald*, January 24, 2017, http://www.miamiherald.com/news/local/article128563889. html (accessed January 30, 2017).
6. Kaylee Joy, comment on the post by Julie Cerel, PhD, "Suicide: Finding Hope," SuicideFindingHope.com, February 11, 2013, http://www.suicidefindinghope.com/content/how_many_ of_us_are_there (accessed November 17, 2016).
7. Cindy Swirko, "Teens Speak Out on Suicide, Intolerance through Poetry," *Gainesville Sun*, February 28, 2015, http://www.gainesville.com/news/20150228/teens-speak-out-on-suicide -intolerance-through-poetry (accessed November 16, 2016).
8. SAMHSA, *A Journey Toward Help and Hope*, 5.
9. See http://livethroughthis.org/the-project/ (accessed November 21, 2016).
10. Megan Rotatori, "I Survived a Suicide Attempt: Megan Rotatori," LiveThroughThis.org, April 15, 2014, http://livethroughthis.org/#/megan-rotatori/ (accessed November 19, 2016).
11. Nathan Pointer, "I Survived a Suicide Attempt: Nathan Pointer," LiveThroughThis.org, April 7, 2014, http://livethroughthis.org/#/nathan-pointer/ (accessed November 21, 2016).
12. Pointer, "I Survived a Suicide Attempt: Nathan Pointer."
13. Niomi Provins, "I Survived a Suicide Attempt: Niomi Provins," LiveThroughThis.org, November 28, 2013, http://livethroughthis.org/#/niomi-provins/ (accessed November 20, 2016).
14. Provins, "I Survived a Suicide Attempt: Niomi Provins."
15. Max Kutner, "Teen Suicide Is Contagious, and the Problem May Be Worse Than We Thought," *Newsweek*, October 28, 2016, http://www.newsweek.com/2016/10/28/teen-sui cide-contagious-colorado-springs-511365.html (accessed November 17, 2016).

16. Eunice McGarrahan, correspondence with the author, November 17, 2016.

17. McGarrahan, correspondence.

18. McGarrahan, correspondence.

19. Brett Thomas, "4 Fort Wayne–Area Teens Die by Suicide in October," Wane.com, November 3, 2016, http://wane.com/2016/11/03/four-area-teens-died-by-suicide-in-month-of -october/ (accessed January 22, 2017).

20. Deborah Serani, "Understanding Survivors of Suicide Loss," *Psychology Today*, November 25, 2013, https://www.psychologytoday.com/blog/two-takes-depression/201311/ understanding-survivors-suicide-loss (accessed November 17, 2016).

21. J. Brent Bill, "My Best Friend Committed Suicide," Devozine.Upperroom.org, n.d., http:// devozine.upperroom.org/articles/best-friend-committed-suicide/ (accessed November 21, 2016).

22. Sue Thoms, "Riley's Story: After Brother's Suicide, Teen Shares How She Deals with Grief, Offers Advice to Those Who Want to Help," MLive.com, May 22, 2011, http://www.mlive .com/health/index.ssf/2011/05/rileys_story_after_brothers_su.html (accessed November 21, 2016).

23. Danielle Campoamor, "What It Feels Like to Lose a Friend to Suicide," *Huffington Post*, August 12, 2015, http://www.huffingtonpost.com/danielle-campoamor/what-it-feels-like -to-lose-a-friend-to-suicide_b_7973920.html (accessed November 21, 2016).

24. Maia Szalavitz, "How Many Drug Overdoses Are Actually Suicides?" Vice.com, February 29, 2016, https://www.vice.com/en_us/article/how-many-drug-overdoses-are-actually-suicides (accessed January 23, 2017).

25. See Centers for Disease Control and Prevention, "Understanding the Epidemic," CDC.gov, n.d., https://www.cdc.gov/drugoverdose/epidemic/ (accessed March 4, 2017).

26. See Centers for Disease Control and Prevention, "Drug Overdose Death Data," CDC.gov, n.d., https://www.cdc.gov/drugoverdose/data/statedeaths.html (accessed March 4, 2017).

27. Tom Kisken, "Heroin Tightens Deadly Grip on County," *Ventura County Star*, last updated November 28, 2016, http://www.vcstar.com/story/news/local/2016/11/26/heroin-tightens -deadly-grip-county/94081652/ (accessed January 23, 2017).

28. U.S. Department of Veterans Affairs, "Suicide and PTSD," PTSD.VA.gov, n.d., http://www .ptsd.va.gov/public/problems/ptsd-suicide.asp (accessed November 22, 2016).

29. U.S. Department of Veterans Affairs, "VA Suicide Prevention Program Facts about Veteran Suicide," VA.gov, July 2016, https://www.va.gov/opa/publications/factsheets/ Suicide_Prevention_FactSheet_New_VA_Stats_070616_1400.pdf (accessed November 22, 2016).

30. Ashley Fantz, "The Uncounted: The Teenager," CNN.com, March 2014, http://www.cnn. com/interactive/2014/03/us/uncounted-suicides/ (accessed March 5, 2017).

31. Fantz, "The Uncounted."

32. Fantz, "The Uncounted."

a. See American Foundation for Suicide Prevention, "Suicide Statistics," AFSP.org, n.d., https://afsp.org/about-suicide/suicide-statistics/ (accessed March 15, 2017).

b. See American Association of Suicidology (AAS), "Warning Signs and Risk Factors," Suicidology.org, n.d., http://www.suicidology.org/ncpys/warning-signs-risk-factors (accessed March 15, 2017).

c. AAS, "Warning Signs and Risk Factors."

Chapter 8

1. Sabrina Dolling, "Farewell Cupcake—A Eulogy to My Little Sister," Write-Out-Loud .com, n.d., http://www.write-out-loud.com/farewell-cupcake-a-eulogy-to-my-little-siste r.html (accessed December 11, 2016).

2. News 8 Web Staff, "Teen Boating Accident Survivor Speaks at Friend's Funeral," WoodTV. com, June 24, 2016, http://woodtv.com/2016/06/24/teen-boating-accident-survivor-speaks -at-friends-funeral/ (accessed March 6, 2017).

3. Joseph Stapansky, "Friends, Family Attend Funeral of Staten Island Teen Who Died from Asthma: 'Today Is about Me Letting Him Go,'" *New York Daily News*, June 10, 2016, http://www.nydailynews.com/new-york/friends-family-attend-funeral-s-teen-died-asthma -article-1.2669011 (accessed March 6, 2017).

4. Dolling, "Farewell Cupcake."

5. See Associated Press and Zoe Szathmary, "'Akyra's Life Was Short and Shining': Youngest Victim of Orlando Massacre, 18, Is Remembered as a Stellar Student and Basketball Player at Her Funeral in Philadelphia," *Daily Mail.com*, last updated June 27, 2016, http://www .dailymail.co.uk/news/article-3658481/Philadelphia-teen-killed-nightclub-massacre -mourned.html (accessed March 27, 2017).

6. Elizabeth Hernandez, "Students, Family Fill Church for Parker Teen Patric Lantz's Fu-neral," *Denver Post*, January 26, 2016, updated April 18, 2016, http://www.denverpost .com/2016/01/26/students-family-fill-church-for-parker-teen-patric-lantzs-funeral/ (ac-cessed May 15, 2017).

7. Bilal Abu Aisha, "Funeral Rites and Regulations in Islam," MissionIslam.com, n.d., https:// www.missionislam.com/knowledge/funeral.htm (accessed January 31, 2017).

8. Momtaz Begum-Hossain, "A Muslim Daughter's Role in Preparing Her Mother for Burial," *Guardian*, October 26, 2013, https://www.theguardian.com/lifeandstyle/2013/oct/26/ muslim-daughter-mother-burial (accessed March 7, 2017).

9. Begum-Hossain, "A Muslim Daughter's Role."

10. Toby Blackstar, interview by Steven T. Turner, "Toby Blackstar Discusses Funeral Customs in Native American Communities," MyASD.com, March 8, 2016, http://www.myasd.com/ post/3102842-article-toby-blackstar-discusses-funeral-customs (accessed December 8, 2016).

11. Blackstar and Turner, "Toby Blackstar Discusses Funeral Customs."

12. Danie Koskan, "Native American Funerals Have Changed but Retain Unique Qualities," *Rapid City Journal*, November 15, 2014, http://rapidcityjournal.com/lifestyles/faith-and -values/native-american-funerals-have-changed-but-retain-unique-qualities/article _1a401652-917b-5368-807e-b24c47b665ff.html (accessed December 8, 2016).

13. Koskan, "Native American Funerals."

14. "Do It Yourself Funerals," NPR.org, December 8, 1997, http://www.npr.org/programs/ death/971208.death.html (accessed May 15, 2017).

15. Terri Peters, "'A Final Tribute': Teens Serve as Pallbearers for Homeless Military Veterans," *Today*, November 7, 2015, http://www.today.com/series/veterans/final-tribute-teens-serve -pallbearers-homeless-military-veterans-t51966 (accessed December 11, 2016).

16. Joan Cary, "Under New Illinois Law, Playing Taps at Vets' Funerals Can Get Teens out of School," *Chicago Tribune*, December 27, 2016, http://www.chicagotribune.com/news/ct -high-school-taps-players-20161224-story.html (accessed March 6, 2017).

17. Cary, "Under New Illinois Law."

a. See West Virginia Division of Culture and History, "Grave Creek Mound," WVCulture.org, n.d., http://www.wvculture.org/history/gravec.html (accessed March 15, 2017).

Chapter 9

1. Veronica Mena, "Why Latino Catholics Celebrate 3 Life Events in Ways That Other Cultures Normally Don't," CatholicCompany.com, January 14, 2016, https://www.catholiccompany .com/getfed/why-latino-catholics-celebrate-life-events/ (accessed January 18, 2017).
2. Mena, "Why Latino Catholics Celebrate."
3. Panagiotis Pentaris, "Culture and Death: A Multicultural Perspective," Academia.edu, 2010, https://www.academia.edu/2057242/Culture_and_Death_A_multicultural_perspective (accessed December 15, 2016).
4. Terri Firma, "Confirmed: Canadian Teen Alex Radita, a Diabetic, Died Due to Parents' Religious Beliefs," Patheos.com, June 4, 2016, http://www.patheos.com/blogs/friendly atheist/2016/06/04/confirmed-diabetic-teen-alex-radita-died-due-to-canadian-parents -religious-beliefs/ (accessed March 15, 2017). See also Sky Palma, "Parents Who Chose Prayer over Insulin for Dead Son 'Prayed for 2 Hours' as Their Child Lay Dying," DeadState .org, June 3, 2016, http://deadstate.org/parents-who-chose-prayer-over-insulin-for-dead -son-prayed-for-2-hours-as-their-child-lay-dying/ (accessed March 15, 2017).
5. Marc D. Angel, trans., "Thirteen Principles of Faith," in *Maimonides—Essential Teachings on Jewish Faith and Ethics: The Book of Knowledge and Thirteen Principles of Faith* (Woodstock, VT: SkyLight Paths Publishing/LongHill Partners, 2012), 151–171.
6. Pearl Gaskin, *I Believe in . . . Christian, Jewish, Muslim Young People Speak about Their Faith* (Chicago: Cricket Books, 2004), 35.
7. Haley MacMillen, "5 Different Religions and How They Deal with Their Dead," Refinery29 .com, February 25, 2015, http://www.refinery29.com/religious-death-beliefs (accessed December 13, 2016).
8. Dr. Elizabeth Macaulay-Lewis, "The Five Pillars of Islam," KhanAcademy.org, n.d., https:// www.khanacademy.org/humanities/world-history/medieval-times/islam-intro/a/the-five -pillars-of-islam (accessed March 7, 2017).
9. See "Buddhism: An Introduction," PBS.org, n.d., http://www.pbs.org/edens/thailand/ buddhism.htm (accessed March 7, 2017).
10. Dharmachari Vishvapani, "A Teenager's Discovery of Buddhism," FreeBuddhistAudio.com, n.d., https://www.freebuddhistaudio.com/texts/othertexts/Vishvapani/FBA96_A_Teenager -s_Discovery_of_Buddhism.pdf (accessed March 15, 2017).
11. Vishvapani, "A Teenager's Discovery of Buddhism."
12. Caryle Murphey, "Most Americans Believe in Heaven . . . and Hell," PewResearch.org, November 10, 2015, http:/www.pewresearch.org/fact-tank/2015/11/10/most-americans -believe-in-heaven-and-hell/ (accessed March 8, 2017).
13. Maggie Fox, "Fewer Americans Believe in God—Yet They Still Believe in Afterlife," NBC News.com, March 21, 2016, http://www.nbcnews.com/better/wellness/fewer-americans -believe-god-yet-they-still-believe-afterlife-n542966 (accessed March 8, 2017).
14. See Judaism 101, "Olam Ha-Be: The Afterlife," JewFAQ.org, http://www.jewfaq.org/ olamhaba.htm (accessed March 8, 2017).

15. Rabbi Evan Moffic, "Do Jews Believe in an Afterlife?" ReformJudiasm.org, May 10, 2012, http://www.reformjudaism.org/blog/2012/05/10/do-jews-believe-afterlife (accessed March 8, 2017).

16. See "Basic Christian Beliefs," ThoughtCo.com, n.d., https://www.thoughtco.com/basic-christian-beliefs-700357 (accessed March 8, 2017).

17. See "Meeting the Spirit: An Introduction to Quaker Beliefs and Practice," CharlestonWV. Quaker.org, n.d., http://charlestonwv.quaker.org/meeting-the-spirit.html (accessed March 8, 2017).

18. See the Bahá'í Faith website, http://www.bahai.org/ (accessed March 8, 2017).

19. See Unitarian Universalist Association, "Beliefs about Life and Death in Unitarian Universalism," UUA.org, n.d., http://www.uua.org/beliefs/what-we-believe/life-death (accessed January 13, 2017).

20. Arlene Hirschfelder and Paulette Molin, *Encyclopedia of Native American Religions: An Introduction* (New York: Checkmark Books/Facts on File, 2001), vii.

21. Hirschfelder and Molin, *Encyclopedia of Native American Religions*, 66.

22. Courtney Rae, "Days of the Dead," *Teen Ink*, n.d., http://www.teenink.com/users/Courtney Rae (accessed March 28, 2017).

23. Marianne Combs, "Teens Honor Day of the Dead at the MIA," *State of the Arts* (blog), October 30, 2009, http://blogs.mprnews.org/state-of-the-arts/2009/10/teens-make-offerings-for-the-day-of-the-dead/ (accessed March 28, 2017).

24. Combs, "Teens Honor Day of the Dead at the MIA."

a. "Zoroastrianism: An ancient religion founded by Zarathushtra," ReligiousTolerance.org, updated January 25, 2012, http://www.religioustolerance.org/zoroastr.htm (accessed March 7, 2017).

b. See "Zoroastrian Funerals," BBC.co.uk, last updated October 2, 2009, http://www.bbc.co.uk/religion/religions/zoroastrian/ritesrituals/funerals.shtml (accessed March 7, 2017).

c. See "About Cryonics," Cryonics.org, n.d., http://www.cryonics.org/index.php/about-us/ (accessed January 17, 2017).

d. Laura Smith-Spark, "UK Teenager Wins Battle to Have Body Cryogenically Frozen," CNN.com, November 18, 2016, http://www.cnn.com/2016/11/18/health/uk-teenager-cryonics-body-preservation/ (accessed January 17, 2017).

e. Smith-Spark, "UK Teenager Wins Battle."

Chapter 10

1. Paul Sullivan, "Among Young Inheritors, an Urge to Redistribute," *New York Times*, March 25, 2013, http://www.nytimes.com/2013/03/26/your-money/inheriting-a-large-trust-fund-and-giving-the-money-away.html (accessed January 27, 2017).

2. Doriane Lambelet Coleman and Philip M. Rosoff, "The Legal Authority of Mature Minors to Consent to General Medical Treatment," *Pediatrics*, March 25, 2013, p. 787, http://pediatrics.aappublications.org/content/pediatrics/131/4/786.full.pdf (accessed December 24, 2016).

3. Cherie Black, "Boy Dies of Leukemia after Refusing Treatment for Religious Reasons," Seattlepi.com, November 28, 2007, http://www.seattlepi.com/local/article/Boy-dies-of-leukemia-after-refusing-treatment-for-1257094.php (accessed December 27, 2016).

4. Julie Wilson, "Texas Teen Suffering from Stage Four Cancer Says No to Chemo, Opts for Green Diet Instead," Natural.News, November 16, 2015 http://www.natural.news/2015 –11–16-texas-teen-suffering-from-stage-four-cancer-says-no-to-chemo-opts-for-green -diet-instead.html (accessed December 26, 2016).

5. See "Types of Wills," Attorneys.com, n.d., http://www.attorneys.com/wills-trusts-and -probate/types-of-wills (accessed December 26, 2016).

6. Edward A. Haman, "What Is Probate Court?" LegalZoom.com, May 2015, https://www .legalzoom.com/articles/what-is-probate-court (accessed December 26, 2016).

7. Ted Thornhill, "Sight Restored, Burns Healed: Teenager Who Died from Accidental Medication Overdose in 2013 Helps 50 People with His Organs, Tendons, Corneas and Skin," *Daily Mail*, May 5, 2015, http://www.dailymail.co.uk/news/article-3068590/Sight-restored-burns -healed-Teenager-died-accidental-medication-overdose-2013-helps-50-PEOPLE-organs -tendons-corneas-skin.html (accessed March 9, 2017).

8. See WCBD and WNCN, "SC Teen Dies in ATV Crash; Her Donated Heart Saves Another Teen Girl," WNCN.com, last updated September 11, 2016, http://wncn.com/2016/09/11/ sc-teen-dies-in-atv-crash-her-donated-heart-saves-another-teen-girl/ (accessed March 9, 2017).

9. See Tribune Media Wire, "Utah Teen Dies Unexpectedly, One Day after Deciding to Donate Her Organs," CBS4Indy.com, December 17, 2016, http://cbs4indy.com/2016/12/17/utah -teen-dies-unexpectedly-one-day-after-deciding-to-donate-her-organs/ (accessed March 9, 2017).

10. Carlee, "I Want to Make a Difference in This World," OrganDonor.gov, n.d., https://www. organdonor.gov/statistics-stories/donation-stories/carlee-heart-recipient.html (accessed December 28, 2016).

11. Patrick, "Patrick Cornea Transplant Recipient," OrganDonor.gov, n.d., https://www.organ-donor.gov/statistics-stories/donation-stories/patrick-cornea-recipient.html (accessed December 28, 2016).

12. Tara Edwards, "Historical Cemetery in Flat Rock Restored after Teen Damages It," WXYZ .com, last updated September 19, 2016, http://www.wxyz.com/news/historical-cemetery -of-the-family-of-revolutionary-war-vet-restored-after-vandalism (accessed March 10, 2017).

13. "Teens Arrested for Dumping Ashes, Vandalizing 50 Graves in Independence Cemetery," WWLTV.com, October 16, 2016, http://www.wwltv.com/news/local/northshore/teens -arrested-for-dumping-ashes-vandalizing-50-graves-in-indepence-cemetery/336019366 (accessed March 9, 2017).

14. Chris Gothner, "Teen, Community Put Finishing Touches on Cemetery Restoration," KOMU.com, August 29, 2015, http://www.komu.com/news/teen-community-put-finishing -touches-on-cemetery-restoration/ (accessed March 9, 2017).

15. See https://www.facebook.com/pg/Lukes-Eagle-Scout-Project-1872836779608251/photos/; see also https://www.youtube.com/watch?v=raBQtLn3wsE (accessed March 10, 2017).

16. Ella Morton, "The New York Interns Spending Their Summer in a Cemetery," Slate.com, August 18, 2015, http://www.slate.com/blogs/atlas_obscura/2015/08/18/the_teen_interns_ at_woodlawn_cemetery_are_learning_how_to_restore_19th_century.html (accessed March 10, 2017).

17. Morton, "The New York Interns."

18. Morton, "The New York Interns."

a. Associated Press, "'Cassie C' Says Cancer's Back after Court Forced Her into Chemo," NBC News.com, April 29, 2015, http://www.nbcnews.com/health/cancer/cassie-c-says-cancer-s -back-after-court-forced-her-n557991 (accessed December 2, 2016).

b. Ross Toback and Julia Marsh, "Daughters Inherit $20M, but There's a Catch," *New York Post*, July 27, 2015, http://nypost.com/2015/07/27/dad-controlling-daughters-hefty -inheritance-from-the-grave/ (accessed March 10, 2017).

Chapter 11

1. Becky Barnicoat, "25 Stories about People's Last Day with Their Pet That'll Make You Cry," BuzzFeed.com, September 5, 2016, https://www.buzzfeed.com/beckybarnicoat/heart breaking-stories-saying-goodbye-to-your-pet?utm_term=.fo2dz0ZgA1#.jt2pL5R1lz (accessed March 11, 2017).

2. Barnicoat, "25 Stories."

3. Barnicoat, "25 Stories."

4. jmac1780, "Wall of Memories," *Teen Ink*, n.d., http://www.teenink.com/nonfiction/memoir/ article/482610/Wall-Of-Memories/ (accessed March 12, 2017).

5. Clarissa Fallis, "My Service Dog, Lynal, Is Much More Than a Companion," Petful.com, September 27, 2012, http://www.petful.com/service-animal/pyschiatric-service-dog/ (accessed May 16, 2017).

6. Fallis, "My Service Dog."

7. Association for Pet Loss and Bereavement, "Aftercare: Pet Cemeteries and Crematories," APLB.org, n.d., http://aplb.org/services/aftercare.php (accessed December 31, 2016).

8. Moira Anderson Allen, "Ten Tips on Coping with Pet Loss," Pet-Loss.net, 2016, http:// pet-loss.net/ (accessed December 31, 2016).

9. See "Pet Abandonment: Statistics," Animal-Rights-Action.com, n.d., http://www.animal -rights-action.com/pet-abandonment.html#Statistics (accessed January 4, 2017).

10. John Metcalf, "Los Angeles Has a Huge Number of Stray Chihuahuas," CityLab.com, February 26, 2016, http://www.citylab.com/design/2016/02/dog-pounds-los-angeles-data-stray -chihuauas/471117/ (accessed January 23, 2017).

11. Michael J. Fox, "Shelters Destroy Millions of Animals Each Year," *Washington Post*, December 3, 2014, https://www.washingtonpost.com/local/shelters-destroy-millions-of -animals-each-year/2014/11/28/1759aef4-702c-11e4-ad12-3734c461eab6_story.html?utm _term=.34ba558ab18a (accessed March 11, 2017).

12. Paul Solotaroff, "The Dog Factory: Inside the Sickening World of Puppy Mills," *Rolling Stone*, January 3, 2017, http://www.rollingstone.com/culture/features/the-dog-factory -inside-the-sickening-world-of-puppy-mills-w457673 (accessed January 4, 2017).

13. Solotaroff, "The Dog Factory."

14. Solotaroff, "The Dog Factory."

15. See "A Closer Look at Puppy Mills," ASPCA.org, n.d., http://www.aspca.org/animal -cruelty/puppy-mills/closer-look-puppy-mills (accessed January 5, 2017).

16. "Why You Should Never Buy a Puppy Online," ASPCA.org, n.d., http://www.aspca.org/ animal-cruelty/puppy-mills/why-you-should-never-buy-puppy-online (accessed January 5, 2017).

17. Rebecca Frankel, "WdotW: Actually, No, There Are No Military Dogs Left Behind," Foreign Policy.com, September 19, 2014, http://foreignpolicy.com/2014/09/19/wdotw-actually-no -there-are-no-military-dogs-left-behind/ (accessed January 1, 2017).

18. James Clark, "Bond Between a Marine and His Dog Continues after Death," Taskand Purpose.com, March 7, 2016, http://taskandpurpose.com/bond-marine-dog-continues -death/ (accessed January 2, 2017).

19. "Heroic Us Marine Corps Service Dog Awarded Top Medal for War Animals," FoxNews .com, April 5, 2016, http://www.foxnews.com/us/2016/04/05/heroic-us-marine-corps -service-dog-awarded-top-medal-for-war-animals.html (accessed January 2, 2017).

20. Maryann Mott, "Dogs May Mourn as Deeply as Humans Do," *U.S. News & World Report*, July 6, 2012, http://health.usnews.com/health-news/news/articles/2012/07/06/dogs-may -mourn-as-deeply-as-humans-do (accessed January 3, 2017).

21. Petra Mayer, "Questions for Barbara J. King, Author of 'How Animals Grieve,'" NPR.org, May 27, 2013, http://www.npr.org/2013/05/27/185815445/questions-for-barbara-j-king -author-of-how-animals-grieve (accessed January 3, 2017).

22. David Gutierrez, "Pet Dogs Go Out of Their Way to Comfort Humans They Sense Are Sick or Depressed," NaturalNews.com, August 23, 2915, http://www.naturalnews.com/050896_ dogs_emotional_intuition_pets.html (accessed January 23, 2017).

23. Michelle Prawirawidjaja, "Cats and Death," *Anthropological Perspectives on Death* (blog), November 5, 2012, https://scholarblogs.emory.edu/gravematters/tag/process-of-death/ (ac-cessed January 24, 2017).

24. David Raven, "'Miracle Cat' Predicts Deaths of 100 People in Nursing Home," *Mirror*, March 30, 2015, http://www.mirror.co.uk/news/world-news/miracle-cat-predicts -deaths-100-5365056 (accessed May 16, 2017).

---

a. Melanie, "Teen Boys Save Abandoned Dog," LifewithDogs.tv, May 29, 2014, http://www .lifewithdogs.tv/2014/05/teen-boys-save-abandoned-dog-left-to-die/ (accessed March 12, 2017).

Chapter 12

1. Kelley, "Live Your Life to the Fullest," ThisIBelieve.org, June 8, 2011, http://thisibelieve .org/essay/101165/ (accessed January 6, 2017).

2. See https://www.brainyquote.com/quotes/quotes/e/epicurus148954.html (accessed March 16, 2017).

3. Kelley, "Live Your Life."

4. Gini, "I Believe in Living Life to Its Fullest," ThisIBelieve.org, March 4, 2011, http://this ibelieve.org/essay/95550/ (accessed January 6, 2017).

5. See National Center for Health Statistics, "Leading Causes of Death," CDC.gov, n.d., https://www.cdc.gov/nchs/fastats/leading-causes-of-death.htm (accessed May 16, 2017).

6. Lenny Bernstein, "U.S. Life Expectancy Will Soon Be On Par with Mexico's and the Czech Republic's," *Washington Post*, February 21, 2017, https://www.washingtonpost.com/news/ to-your-health/wp/2017/02/21/us-life-expectancy-will-soon-be-on-par-with-mexicos-and -croatias/?utm_term=.d31e73fb8b3e (accessed May 16, 2017).

7. See Celes, "101 Ways to Live Your Life to the Fullest," *Personal Excellence* (blog), n.d., https://personalexcellence.co/blog/101-ways-to-live-your-life-to-the-fullest/ (accessed March 13, 2017).

8. Caroline Gregoire, "The 75-Year Study That Found the Secrets to a Fulfilling Life," *Huffington Post*, last updated August 23, 2013, http://www.huffingtonpost.com/2013/08/11/how-this-harvard-psycholo_n_3727229.html (accessed May 16, 2017).

9. Karl Moore, "Millennials Work for Purpose, Not Paycheck," *Forbes*, October 2, 2014, http://www.forbes.com/sites/karlmoore/2014/10/02/millennials-work-for-purpose-not-paycheck/#5b6cdab85a22 (accessed January 14, 2017).

10. Khatijah Arif, "Life as a Muslim Teenager," BBC.co.uk, September 10, 2008, http://www.bbc.co.uk/southyorkshire/content/articles/2008/09/10/ramadan_muslim_women_feature.shtml (accessed March 14, 2017).

11. Fizzah Abbasi, "As a Muslim American Teen, I Shouldn't Have to Live in Fear," *Huffington Post: The Blog*, last updated May 4, 2015, http://www.huffingtonpost.com/fizzah-abbasi/as-a-muslim-american-teen-i-shouldnt-have-to-live-in-fear_b_6787616.html (accessed January 26, 2017).

12. Marilyn A., "Real Life: Purpose," EveryStudent.com, n.d., www.everystudent.com/features/reallife.html (accessed January 17, 2017).

13. Marilyn A., "Real Life."

14. Teen reporters from the *Mash*, "Teens Navigate Their Own Paths When It Comes to Religion," *Huffington Post: The Blog*, last updated October 26, 2016, http://www.huffingtonpost.com/the-mash/teens-navigate-their-own_b_8394484.html; see also http://themash.com/blog/news/2015/10/26/good-faith/ (accessed March 13, 2017).

15. Teen reporters, "Teens Navigate."

16. Teen reporters, "Teens Navigate."

17. Teen reporters, "Teens Navigate."

18. Pearl Gaskin, *I Believe In . . . Christian, Jewish, Muslim Young People Speak about Their Faith* (Chicago: Cricket Books, 2004), 114–15.

19. Aubriel_J, "Discussion: by Aubriel J.," RichardDawkins.net, May 20, 2013, https://richarddawkins.net/2013/05/atheist-teen/ (accessed March 14, 2017).

20. Ryan Stringer, "Yes, Life without Religion Can Be Meaningful," *Huffington Post: The Blog*, March 8, 2016, http://www.huffingtonpost.com/ryan-stringer/yes-life-without-religion-can-be-meaningful_b_9376188.html (accessed January 11, 2017).

21. Michael Lipka, "Why America's 'Nones' Left Religion Behind," PewResearch.org, August 24, 2016, http://www.pewresearch.org/fact-tank/2016/08/24/why-americas-nones-left-religion-behind/ (accessed March 14, 2017).

22. Isaac Saul, "You're Not Agnostic, You're an Atheist," *Huffington Post: The Blog*, March 29, 2014, http://www.huffingtonpost.com/isaac-saul/youre-not-agnostic-youre-an-atheist_b_4675638.html (accessed May 16, 2017).

23. Michaela Shelley, "This Is What It's Like to Be a Teen Living with a Chronic Illness," *Huffington Post: The Blog*, April 8, 2015, http://www.huffingtonpost.com/michaela-shelley/this-is-what-its-like-to-be-a-teen-living-with-a-chronic-illness_b_6898318.html (accessed January 9, 2016).

24. ADMIN, "Terminally Ill Teen Starts Animal Rescue," LifewithDogs.tv, March 11, 2014, http://www.lifewithdogs.tv/2014/03/terminally-ill-teen-starts-animal-rescue/ (accessed January 9, 2016).

25. Erin Grace, "Teen with Cancer Strives to 'Live a Better Life'—and Wants Us All to Do the Same," Omaha.com, November 7, 2016, http://www.omaha.com/livewellnebraska/health/ grace-teen-with-cancer-strives-to-live-a-better-life/article_d29dee5d-c273-53ba-b70a -bf8cfd9fbb9a.html (accessed January 10, 2017).

26. Grace, "Teen with Cancer."

27. Matthew Hutson, "Everyday Routines Make Life Seem More Meaningful," Scientific American.com, July 1, 2015, https://www.scientificamerican.com/article/everyday-routines -make-life-feel-more-meaningful/ (accessed January 16, 2017).

28. Susan Krauss Whitbourne, "Fulfillment at Any Age," *Psychology Today*, September 21, 2010, https://www.psychologytoday.com/blog/fulfillment-any-age/201009/seeking-long-term -fulfillment-not-happiness-will-get-you-through (accessed March 14, 2017).

29. For the full transcript of Obama's speech, see http://www.npr.org/2017/01/10/509137106/ watch-live-obama-addresses-the-nation-in-farewell-speech, time.com/4631007/president -obama-farewell-speech-transcript/, or http://www.latimes.com/politics/la-pol-obama -farewell-speech-transcript-20170110-story.html.

---

a. Pew Forum, "Religion in Everyday Life," PewForum.org, April 12, 2016, http://www.pew forum.org/2016/04/12/religion-in-everyday-life/ (accessed January 12, 2017).

Further Reading

Books

Bowen, James. *A Street Cat Named Bob and How He Saved My Life*. New York: Thomas Nunne Books/St. Martin's Press, 2012.

Cefrey, Holly and Randall McPartland. *HIV and AIDS Deadliest Diseases of All Time*. New York: Cavendish Square Publishing, 2016.

Friedman, Russell, Cole James, and John W. James. *The Grief Recovery Handbook for Pet Loss*. Lanham, MD: Rowman & Littlefield, 2014.

Grollman, Earl A. *A Teen's Guide to Coping with Grief and Finding Meaning after Loss*. Boston: Beacon Press, 2014.

Hyatt, Erica Goldblatt. *Grieving for the Sibling You Lost: A Teen's Guide to Coping with Grief and Finding Meaning after Loss*. Oakland, CA: New Harbinger Publications, 2015.

Kübler-Ross, Elizabeth. *On Death and Dying*. New York: Macmillan, 2007.

Mayshark, Loren. *Death: An Exploration: Learning to Embrace Life's Most Feared Mystery*. Bemus Point, NY: Red Scorpion Press, 2016.

Neumann, Ann. *The Good Death: An Exploration of Dying in America*. Boston: Beacon Press, 2016.

Substance Abuse and Mental Health Services Administration. *A Journey Toward Help and Hope: Your Handbook for Recovery after a Suicide Attempt*. Rockville, MD: U.S. Department of Health and Human Services, 2015.

Vogelsang, Jessica. *All Dogs Go to Kevin: Everything Three Dogs Taught Me That I Didn't Learn in Veterinary School*. New York: Grand Central Publishing, 2015.

Websites

American Association of Suicidology: www.suicidology.org.

Arlington National Cemetery: www.arlingtoncemetery.mil. Arlington is considered the nation's most hallowed ground.

Encyclopedia of Death and Dying: www.deathreference.com.

Final Exit Network: www.finalexitnetwork.org. The network for a world federation that focuses on the right to die.

GirlsHealth.gov: www.girlshealth.gov. This site covers nutrition, fitness, relationships, bullying, and other health issues.

Life in the USA: www.lifeintheusa.com. This site is a web guide to American life for immigrants and Americans.

Live Through This: www.livethroughthis.org. The website provides a collection of portraits and stories of suicide attempt survivors, as told by those survivors.

Mayo Clinic: www.mayoclinic.org. Mayo Clinic's website provides much information about health issues as well as terminal illness.

National Cancer Institute: www.cancer.gov.

National Center for Biotechnology Information: www.ncbi.nlm.nih.gov.

Suicide Finding Hope: www.suicidefindinghope.com. This website can help you find information about suicide, mental illness, or coping with suicide loss.

TeenHelp: www.teenhelp.org. This site provides an online place to connect with thousands of teenagers worldwide.

Teen Ink: www.teenink.com. *Teen Ink* is a magazine and Internet site written by and for teens.

Unitarian Universalist Association: www.uua.org.

U.S. Centers for Disease Control and Prevention: www.cdc.gov.

Write-Out-Loud.com: www.write-out-loud.com. This site provides information to help people speak up and let their voices be heard.

Index

About the Author

Kathlyn Gay is the author of more than 120 nonfiction books for children, teenagers, and adults. Her work focuses on diverse subjects, including social, environmental, and multicultural issues and history. She has done extensive research on numerous topics for her wide variety of books, which reviewers call "factual, well-organized, straightforward, and readable." Kathlyn has also authored/edited several encyclopedias. She is the author of a number of titles in the It Happened to Me series:

- *Epilepsy: The Ultimate Teen Guide*, second edition (2017)
- *Activism: The Ultimate Teen Guide* (2016)
- *Divorce: The Ultimate Teen Guide* (2014)
- *Bigotry and Intolerance: The Ultimate Teen Guide* (2013)
- *Living Green: The Ultimate Teen Guide* (2012)
- *Body Image and Appearance: The Ultimate Teen Guide* (2009)
- *The Military and Teens: The Ultimate Teen Guide* (2008)
- *Religion and Spirituality in America: The Ultimate Teen Guide* (2006)
- *Volunteering: The Ultimate Teen Guide* (2004)
- *Cultural Diversity: The Ultimate Teen Guide* (2003)